ME

RICKY MARTIN
ME

A CELEBRA BOOK

Celebra
Published by New American Library, a division of
Penguin Group (USA) Inc., 375 Hudson Street,
New York, New York 10014, USA
Penguin Group (Canada), 90 Eglinton Avenue East, Suite 700, Toronto,
Ontario M4P 2Y3, Canada (a division of Pearson Penguin Canada Inc.)
Penguin Books Ltd., 80 Strand, London WC2R 0RL, England
Penguin Ireland, 25 St. Stephen's Green, Dublin 2,
Ireland (a division of Penguin Books Ltd.)
Penguin Group (Australia), 250 Camberwell Road, Camberwell, Victoria 3124,
Australia (a division of Pearson Australia Group Pty. Ltd.)
Penguin Books India Pvt. Ltd., 11 Community Centre, Panchsheel Park,
New Delhi - 110 017, India
Penguin Group (NZ), 67 Apollo Drive, Rosedale, North Shore 0632,
New Zealand (a division of Pearson New Zealand Ltd.)
Penguin Books (South Africa) (Pty.) Ltd., 24 Sturdee Avenue,
Rosebank, Johannesburg 2196, South Africa

Penguin Books Ltd., Registered Offices:
80 Strand, London WC2R 0RL, England

Published by Celebra, an imprint of New American Library,
a division of Penguin Group (USA) Inc.

First Printing, November 2010
10 9 8 7 6 5 4 3 2 1

LIBRARY OF CONGRESS CATALOGING-IN-PUBLICATION DATA:

Martin, Ricky.
Me/Ricky Martin.
  p. cm.
ISBN 978-0-451-23415-5
1. Martin, Ricky. 2. Singers—Biography. I. Title.
ML420.M3323A3 2010
782.42164092—dc22
[B]   2010034364

Set in Sabon
Designed by Pauline Neuwirth

Printed in the United States of America

PUBLISHER'S NOTE
Penguin is committed to publishing works of quality and integrity. In that spirit, we are proud to offer this book to our readers; however the story, the experiences and the words are the author's alone.
    Publisher does not have any control over and does not assume any responsibility for author or third-party Web sites or their content.

Dedicated to Matteo and Valentino Martin

My light, my focus, my strength, my little masters,
who, with just a simple gaze, know how to tell me,
"Don't worry, Daddy. Everything is okay."

CONTENTS

ME

INTRODUCTION

God, help me to tell the truth to the strong and to avoid telling lies to get the weak's applause. If you give me fortune, do not take away my reason. If you give me success, do not take away my humility. If you give me humility, do not take away my dignity. God, help me to see the other side of the medal. Don't let me blame others of treason just because they don't think like me. God, teach me to love people as I love myself and to judge me as I judge others. Please, don't let me be proud if I succeed, or fall in despair if I fail. Remind me that failure is the experience that precedes triumph. Teach me that forgiving is the most important in the strong and that revenge is the most primitive sign in the weak. If you take away my success, let me keep my strength to succeed from failure. If I fail people, give me courage to apologize and if people fail me, give me courage to forgive them. God, if I forget you, please do not forget me.

—MAHATMA GANDHI

GANDHI'S WORDS TOUCH MY HEART.
At some point in our lives, all of us ultimately arrive at a moment when we are somehow compelled to look back

and consciously reflect on the life we have led. We feel the need to understand where we come from, because we want to see with more clarity where we are actually headed and where it is that we really want to go; we search for a way to balance that which we have lived and that which remains for us to experience, with the desire, perhaps, to find a more meaningful purpose to our existence. Some people decide to do this when they are older, closer to the end of their lives, but for me this moment is right now. Today I feel the need to look back and observe the path that has led me to where I am, so that the future that lies ahead can be as luminous and truthful as possible.

MY GIVEN NAME is Enrique Martin Morales, but most people know me as Ricky Martin: musician, singer, composer, philanthropist, and some might also know I'm an actor. And I am all of those things; but I am also a lot more. The people closest to me know me as "Kiki" (a nickname that comes from Enrique), and aside from being an artist I am also a son, a brother, a friend—and most recently, a father. For so long I tried to keep those parts of my life completely separate: When I am onstage or in front of the cameras, I am "Ricky"; but in private I am "Kiki," a man who each day confronts the challenges of life, just like everybody else. While most people reading this book have a clear sense of who I am as an artist, there is a fundamental part of me that very few really know.

Today, after all that I have lived and the many experiences I have been through, I realize that it isn't fair to separate "Kiki" from "Ricky." They are one and the same. It has taken me some time to understand this, and although I used to believe that the best thing would be to hide my personal life and the essence of who I am, now I hold the full conviction that my true happiness lies in living my life freely, without any fears or false pretexts. It has been a gradual process. I can't say exactly when the realization hit me, but I do know that I got to the point where I could no longer live without facing my truth. This is why I have chosen to finally end the secret that I have carefully guarded for so many years: I have decided to tell the world that I accept my homosexuality and celebrate this gift that life has given me.

Now I feel strong. Free. More free than ever.

Many people probably believe that my life can be broken down into two periods: before and after "Livin' La Vida Loca." Or maybe there are some who think my life is divided between the before and after of my revelation, and the truth is that this is completely understandable, because until now, that's more or less all I have really shared about myself. And though I won't deny the fact that "Livin' La Vida Loca" was a critical moment in my life, I can guarantee that there were many others equally as important to me. There are also the before and after of Menudo, the before and after of my first trip to India, and the before and after of becoming a father. . . . They have all been unique experiences that have impacted me profoundly and altered the way I navigate life. And I hope—*I know*—that there are many more such moments still to come.

Just like everyone else, I have had to walk down my own spiritual path and live through my experiences—the good and the bad, the love and the lack of love, the sense of feeling lost and then finding myself—to arrive at where I am today. Before I could begin to answer the endless questions that were constantly asked of me, I needed to face myself. Of course, some might say I should have done this many years ago, but in the deepest part of my being, I am certain that the moment is now, because that is how it was always meant to be. It is only now that I am ready, and it is only now that I can do it—not one day earlier or one day later.

The process of writing this memoir has not been easy. It has demanded a lot from me—above and beyond what I expected. I've had to tie up loose ends that I'd never attempted to tie up before, to work deeply into memories that were already erased from my mind, and to find answers to very difficult questions; but above all else . . . above everything, I have finally had to accept myself. I have had to bare myself utterly and completely to see myself exactly as I am. I discovered things that I liked—and others not as much. And it was precisely the things I didn't like so much that I became intent on remedying from the moment I became conscious of them. I would have never imagined that writing this book would lead me to where it has; however, today I know that I am a better man—and a happier man—because of what I have learned about myself throughout the process.

I wanted to say a lot in these pages, but I wanted to do it with humility and dignity, focusing on the experiences that have helped shape me. More than an autobiography, this book is a testament of my spiritual beliefs, an account of the steps I have taken to arrive at the place of happiness and completeness where I now find myself. I'll talk about many personal matters that I have never discussed publicly before, but it isn't my intention to share every little thing, either. I believe that we're all entitled to a certain degree of privacy; there are certain things I keep to myself because they are mine alone and I want them to stay that way. What I would like to do is explore the different paths and experiences that have led me to be the person I am today.

I know what it feels like to be loved and I know what it feels like to love someone—totally and absolutely, with intensity and without any prejudgments. I also know what it is like to be judged for what I am and for what I am not. If I hadn't gone through all of this, maybe I wouldn't have been able to arrive at the moment when I finally understood that my chosen path was the right one, since it has made me into the person I am today. And it doesn't matter how I look at it; that person I am today, that person I have created with so much effort and dedication, is, second to my children, my most precious work. I am certain that there are many more steps left for me to take, many more things to experience, and therefore many chapters left to write. But right now I just want to open my heart to you and share my story and this moment of my life with the world.

During this time I have learned that it is useless to label things as either good or bad. The key is to see everything as a lesson. Good and bad alike are both part of a whole, and we have to embrace that whole to reach the complete existence we long for. We advance on certain paths where opportunities come our way, and every step not only gets us closer to where we want to go but also has a reason for being. Life gives us experiences, and every decision we make determines where we will be later.

From the day we are born until the day we die, we progress on a path of learning, in which every decision we make or fail to make becomes a part of our personal growth. There is this karmic realm where you have to pass through the challenges that life gives you to liberate yourself from that which weighs you down, preventing you from reaching divinity. We all progress down a spiritual path that offers us opportunities to learn—and even tragedy has its meaning. When you're a student, you have to study the lesson until you know it by heart, and if you don't know it, you don't graduate. In the same way, life presents us with experience after experience, and with every deed, decision, and selection we are determining where we will end up. And just like in school, whoever pays the closest attention will most quickly move ahead.

Someone once asked me if I thought my accomplishments were always in my destiny. The answer was yes, and no. Granted, I do believe that a lot of what has happened to me has helped shape my destiny, but there is no doubt that I have come to where I am, and accomplished what I have, because I worked hard to get it. If anything is true in this world it is that destiny is something you have to help. If I had not done my own part, I would have never come to where I am now. At no point did I sit down and wait for destiny to show up on my doorstep. I went out and looked for it and knocked on its door instead. I think that the people who sit around and wait for their destiny to land in their laps will probably get old waiting.

I have worked intensely to arrive at this point, which is why I know it has not been a coincidence or a simple act of randomness. It is true that I have had a lot of luck—or a lot of what we call luck. But the truth is that everyone creates his own luck and his own destiny. When life presents you with a river, you cannot rely on luck to supply a boat; you have to dive into the water and swim. Stroke after stroke, you have to reach the other side. You have to create the course of your own destiny and not let chance determine your direction. I fully believe that luck comes to those who have worked hard to find it.

Life is a journey and every step we take moves us in some direction. When we are ready and willing, we learn, we advance, and we grow. But it's very easy—and very common—to not take that first step and to stay exactly where we are, because after all, that which is familiar is usually the most comfortable. I think that for a great part of my life I was so comfortable I did not feel the need to look inward, even for the sake of asking myself some basic questions—never mind finding the answers. I felt bad. I knew there was something fundamentally wrong inside, but instead of trying to heal these contradictory feelings that nagged at me, I simply buried them with the hope that they would disappear forever. I was afraid and I was much more concerned with being accepted and being liked than with the cultivation of my own personal growth.

The long road to finally come face-to-face with myself has not been easy. And though I've grown and learned a lot, it is a road I continue to tread upon every day of my life. I needed many years of silence and reflection to understand what it is I truly carry in my heart. Before I could tell my truth to the world, I had to come to a moment when I would find inner acceptance and tranquillity.

Life takes lots of twists and turns, but today I have the absolute certainty that everything happens for a reason. Sometimes it is hard to see it when you are the one going through it, but based on my own life, I can say that everything happens because that is the way it has to be. Life's lessons are like a series of closed doors: Upon gaining the insight and learning the relevant lesson, one door closes and another one opens, and you continue your journey. Every phase of my life has brought along valuable and important things; it does not matter how much it has cost me or how difficult it's been. My experiences with Menudo, for example, gave me a work ethic and a sense of discipline that perhaps back then I did not realize would be so crucial in my future. Later, after the chaos of "Livin' La Vida Loca" subsided, I had finally learned about the importance of knowing when to say no. When I went to India, I learned about what it means to turn my gaze inward and know myself. As a new father (and like all fathers before me), I have only recently learned the true significance of unconditional love. And when I finally found the courage to reveal my truth to the world, I not only understood the meaning of living without fear, but I finally understood that fear is truly all in our heads.

As I wrote this book I went through so many moments when I felt completely vulnerable. But at the same time there were other moments when I felt excited, free, and happy to at last let go of my past. It has been an intense process of catharsis that has helped me to heal many wounds and understand many things that perhaps back then did not seem to make sense. Now I see things more clearly, and for that I am grateful.

Now I am complete.

Now I am ready to give myself exactly as I am—to my public, to my family, to my friends and my relationships. I want my children to be able to read this book one day and understand the spiritual journey I had to experience to be able to accept the joy of being their father. I want to open my heart to them fully and absolutely so that in the future they will never be afraid to do the same.

I wrote this book with my heart on my sleeve. But before I continue, I want to clarify that just because I have chosen to talk about my own life does not mean I will talk about the lives of others. Everyone has a right to their privacy and discretion, which is why I have decided to protect the real names and characteristics of certain people. Even though there are some people who have formed part of my public life, and who are likely easily recognizable, I won't involve them in this history that is not theirs. Just as I have asked for my right to privacy on so many occasions, I must respect others' rights to theirs. This is my life, my personal trajectory, and I have decided to tell it because today I am ready to do it. But I don't plan to let my decision affect anyone else.

From the moment I clicked SEND to announce my truth to the world, the rain of love that I've received has been astounding, almost startling. It has shown me clearly that the fear I felt before existed only in my head—as does all fear. Life is so much more beautiful when you live it with open arms, your guard dropped, and without anxieties or secrets. Today, more than ever, I know that this is my moment, and that, just as the master Gandhi says it, I have the strength to live a life filled with love, peace, and truth.

ONE
BECOMING A MAN

IT IS FASCINATING FOR ME TO SIT AND LOOK BACK AT THE road I have traveled to get to where I am now—not only in my career, but in my personal life as well. What has at times felt incomprehensible or excessively difficult, today I understand as something that had to happen. All my experiences have prepared me for what was—and still is—ahead of me. At first it was a difficult concept for me to grasp, but once I was able to internalize it, I got to a point where I could live a more complete and satisfactory life because I am willing to accept that the good, the bad, and the not so great are all part of a whole. This feeling has liberated me in so many ways and given me the strength to confront everything that comes my way. It is extraordinary to think that without knowing it, from very early on, I was already building my identity, my very own story.

GETTING STARTED

It ALL BEGAN with a spoon.

Anybody in my family will tell you that music came into my life at a very young age. My mother's side of the family has always been musically inclined. On Sunday afternoons we would get together at my grandparents' house, and sooner or later someone would pull out a guitar and start singing. My grandfather, for example, was a poet, a good one. His rhymed improvisations were romantic and very stylized, in a way I have never heard again. My grandfather was a firm man, very conservative, and completely devoted to his family. Like most men of his generation he was very macho, but if there is one thing he taught all of us men who carry his name, it is the importance of showing respect to a woman, the beauty of admiring her, caring for her, and protecting her. He would always say to us: "A woman must be treated with the subtle delicacy that you would give to a rose petal." He was obviously a hopeless romantic, a quality that I have, without a doubt, inherited.

From the time I was six years old, I would grab a wooden kitchen spoon and use it as a microphone to sing. I would spend hours upon hours with the spoon in my hand, interpreting my favorite songs—Menudo songs, or songs from American rock bands, such as REO Speedwagon, Journey, and Led Zeppelin, which is what my older siblings were listening to at the time. I remember many times we were all at my grandparents' house, and while everyone was sitting on the balcony getting a breath of fresh air and telling stories, I would put some music on, take hold of my "microphone," and start to sing.

I have no doubt that back then no one ever imagined I'd end up becoming a professional artist (although I did have an uncle who always said, "When you get famous, call me and I'll come carry your luggage." To which I would very seriously reply, "Of course!" Needless to say, he hasn't come through with his end of the bargain . . .). I'm sure they enjoyed watching me sing and dance around the house, but I know it never occurred to any of us that one day I would be doing just that before hundreds of thousands of people.

As surprising as it may seem, the truth is that ever since I was a young boy, I have always known I was meant to be onstage. I can't say it was a conscious decision or that I woke up one day and said, "I want to be an artist." But I can say that I gradually started to realize what I really enjoy doing, and simply tried to do it as often as possible. I know it takes some people many years to figure out what they want to do with their lives, to find something that genuinely moves them, and I know it can be a difficult process. But I was lucky. For me, it was very instinctive. Although at first all I did was grab the spoon and perform for my grandparents and aunts and uncles, I enjoyed it very much. In this case, I believe it was more than a passing phase; it was something more powerful, because what started as a game ultimately turned into a passion. Slowly, I started to see that capturing other people's attention and having all those eyes on me was a rush. I loved feeling that I was entertaining them, that they were listening to me, and when I got big applause, I'd be thrilled to no end. To this very day that feeling of being onstage continues to be a source of energy and inspiration for me. Every time I find myself in front of an audience, be it twenty people or one hundred thousand, once again I feel the energy that consumed me back at the family gatherings of my youth.

I am not exactly sure where my passion for being onstage comes from, but it somehow feels like I have to be in the spotlight; I want to be seen. . . . At some point during my childhood one of my cousins would produce plays—written by her—and it is there where I had my first experiences as an actor. My cousin was no older than eight or nine, but she was incredibly brilliant for her age. Apparently I liked it, because later when I was in school, each time they put on a play I was the first one to sign up. I even became an altar boy, because to me, helping the priest was like being onstage, since he was very much "the star" of the show. When I was onstage I felt complete and alive, so naturally I wanted to find that sensation at every opportunity.

Every so often I think about what would have happened if I had not chosen this path. It's almost inevitable to ask yourself these questions, and it's interesting to think about what would have become of each of our lives if we hadn't turned into the people we are today. What would I be had I not become an artist? What other profession would I have chosen? Psychologist? Dentist? Lawyer? My grandmother had always hoped that I'd be a doctor, but unfortunately I could never fulfill that dream. Since the moment I realized what I wanted to do with myself, I've worked tirelessly to make that dream come true. But I always ask myself what would have become of me had I listened to my grandmother's advice, or had I taken some other path. For example, when I was eighteen, I auditioned for the Tisch School at New York University, one of the most renowned drama schools in the country. But just a few months before classes began, instead of enrolling I went to Mexico to meet some friends, and there I landed—there really is no other way of seeing it, as it was such a coincidence—in the theater.

What would have happened if I had stayed to go to New York University? What direction would my life have taken if I had found success in acting instead of music? My path would have, without a doubt, been different. But I like to think that whether I had chosen acting, music, or dance, I would have somehow or other always chosen a path that in the end would make me feel happy and fulfilled. The truth is that what you do doesn't matter so much; what matters is that you love it and that you do it to the best of your ability.

Passion is a vital aspect of my existence. I consider myself to be a realistic dreamer, and my life is full of intense emotions. I live and feel deeply. Some people may think it is wrong to live life so passionately, but the truth is that ever since I was a very little boy, it has been passion that has propelled me on the extraordinary trajectory that has been my life, so I see no reason to stop it. Had I not embraced my instincts at a very young age, I think I would have never gotten to where I am today. To me, part of the beauty of childhood lies in the fact that it is a time of extremes: When we are happy, the happiness is absolute, and when we are sad, the pain is devastating. Life at that age is very intense, but at the same time it is also utterly pure and genuine. As we grow up, we learn how to soothe the emotions that are too overwhelming, and though to a certain degree I've also had to grow up, I have always made an effort to stay in touch with my inner child—that passionate, energetic, and happy child who was never afraid of anything.

ABUELA

MY PARENTS SEPARATED when I was two years old. Needless to say I remember nothing of what was going on in my life at the time that happened, but I do know that I started spending a great deal of time with my grandparents on both my mother's and my father's sides. My grandparents played a key role in my life. I don't know if it's cultural or simply spiritual, but my relationship with them was always—and continues to be—very important to me. I will never forget what they taught me, and I will strive to pass their teaching on to my sons.

My paternal grandmother was an intelligent woman, independent and confident, a woman who was well ahead of her time. She was into metaphysics long before it became fashionable. She was also an artist; she painted and made sculptures. I remember her as always being busy, doing one of the thousands of things that interested her. She didn't understand the concept of "staying still" and always had some kind of project going on. My great-grandmother— her mother—was a teacher, so my grandmother was practically raised in a classroom, listening to her mother's lectures. She graduated from high school at fourteen, and even wrote two books and became a senior professor at the University of Puerto Rico. Remember, we are talking about a time when society dictated that most women could only aspire to be mothers or housewives. She was a surprising woman, so brave and such a visionary, that one day she decided to pack her bags and move to Boston to study education. In those times! But she moved to Boston and lived there until she graduated with a degree.

I recently had the opportunity to dine with Sonia Sotomayor, the first Latina judge of the United States Supreme Court, and when I told her about my grandmother's accomplishments, she was shocked. "A Latina woman studying in Boston in the forties? Your grandmother must have been a strong woman," she said. And I of course felt very proud, because she was right: My grandmother was definitely an incredible lady.

Although she was born in Puerto Rico, my grandmother's family was originally from Corsica. We Corsicans are famous for being stubborn, and my grandmother was no exception: She was a very strong woman who was never afraid of anything. To me, she was always an example of what it means to be strong. For example, after fifty-some years of marriage, she realized she was no longer feeling fulfilled, so one day she got up and said to my grandfather: "You know what? I want a divorce." In those days people got married for life, "until death do us part." It wasn't like today, when people get divorced for almost any reason at all. But my grandmother didn't care what other people thought or said. For whatever reason, she wasn't happy and she decided to do something about it. So my grandparents got divorced. After that, my grandfather would visit her every day, but the new domestic agreement remained, with her living in her own home, and him separately in his.

My grandmother passed away more than ten years ago, after having lived a long, full life, well into her old age, and if there is anything I am grateful for, it is that she lived long enough to see and be a part of my success. Once, she even got on a plane and came to see me perform on Broadway when I was doing *Les Misérables* in New York. And let me tell you, she was definitely not a fan of airplanes! She once told me that she was terribly afraid of them since the day she flew back to Puerto Rico after finishing her studies in Boston. Apparently, there was some kind of electrical storm during the flight and the plane shook intensely. From that day on, she vowed she would never get on a plane again! And so it was. She only traveled by boat, that trip to New York being the one exception.

It makes me sad to think I wasn't able to see more of her during her last few years. I was working so much, always coming or going, always running, never having enough time to do the things that really matter. I did get to see her every now and then, in passing, but never again did I have the chance to spend days or weeks at a time with her, the way I did when I was a little boy. I remember one time I went to see her accompanied by a police escort. When I arrived at her house with the security unit, I yelled: "Grandma, I'm here to see you!"

"Oh, son!" she said. "How wonderful!"

But right away I had to clarify: "I've come to see you, Grandma, but I can't stay too long. I have to go soon." Like always, she didn't make me feel guilty about having to leave. She simply thanked me for the visit and gave me a great big hug.

"Okay," she said, "it was wonderful to see you. Eat, you're too skinny."

That was my grandmother.

Another time, when I was on a trip in Puerto Rico, I had a helicopter land in her neighborhood's baseball field just to see her. It was the only way I could do it because I had no time. While en route from one side of the island to the other on a business matter, I suddenly told the pilot: "I have to see my grandmother. Land in that baseball field!"

And just like that, I got to spend another moment with her.

There is nothing like grandmothers. To this day her teachings continue to serve me well. Some of the sweetest memories I have of my grandmother are of the two of us sitting there, me doing my homework and her painting or working on one of her projects. I often think of her wise words and her advice and feel as though I somehow carry her inside me. It's such a blessing to be able to feel her so close.

The only thing that does pain me when I think of her is that she never got to meet my children. There are so many things about her that I would have wanted them to know, and no matter how much I tell them about her, I feel that I will never be able to fully explain. For example, when I was younger, she would sing this beautiful lullaby to my cousins and me. I often close my eyes and try to remember it, but I become frustrated because I can't. I can perfectly recall the tone of her voice and the expression on her face as she sang to us, but no matter how hard I try, I simply cannot remember the lyrics or the melody of that song. I just can't. So I pray that this song will one day come back to me in a dream. I ask: "Dear God, Grandma, wherever you may be, if this is true or not, if you exist or not, if you are there or not, please remind me of that song. I want to sing it to my children."

It has not come yet, but I have not lost hope. I know that the afterlife exists, and that she is watching me with a great big smile on her face, because she can see that her first grandson walks through life with the same determination that she possessed, being a strong and independent man, just as she raised me to be.

A TASTE OF FAME

MY FAMILY ALWAYS supported me when I began my artistic career. They came to recognize that music was more than just a game for me. Seeing that I was so passionate about it, they encouraged me to follow it, and that alone gave me a lot of strength: The simple fact that they believed in me gave me a lot of security and nourished my self-esteem. This is why it was no surprise to them when I started doing television commercials in Puerto Rico at the age of nine.

One day, an ad ran in the newspaper saying, "Agency seeking talent for TV commercials." My father read it and asked me, "What do you think?" I thought it was a great idea, so I answered: "Let's do it, Papi, let's go!" That very Saturday we went to the audition. The audition was just to see if the head of the agency would even accept me, and from that moment on, I would start going out on auditions for the actual television commercials. They stood me in front of a camera, asked what my name was, my age, and which school I attended, and honestly, I don't remember what else. I suppose they had me act or read something . . . Maybe they gave me a small scene, the typical things they have you do at an audition. What I do remember well is that I felt very confident. I was not nervous at all. When I finished I returned home, and just days later I was called up again for my first audition.

The first commercial I did was for a soft drink. It was four days of shooting, four intense days, because they would start at six a.m. and end late in the afternoon. Unfortunately, I never got to see the commercial because it was for the U.S. Latino audience and Mexico. But what I do recall is that at the end of it all, they paid me $1,300. And that was not all; every six months I would receive another check for $900 (residuals). It was an amazing job! I was doing something I genuinely enjoyed, and on top of it all I was getting paid well—I couldn't have imagined anything better. A whole new world had opened itself to me.

Many more commercials would soon follow: one for a toothpaste, one for a fast-food restaurant. . . . One commercial would lead to the next one, and the next one, and the next. Once I was in the game, the opportunities started cropping up, and in a year and a half I had done eleven commercials, which I know thanks to my father, who has them all written down! It was so long ago that if it were not for his meticulous record keeping, I would never be able to remember them all. I had a lot of success doing commercials, and after a while I started to become recognized in the field. Since I already had experience and I loved being in front of the cameras, the producers were always inclined to cast me, and that of course kept giving me even more confidence and experience.

Those commercials gave me my first brush with fame. When I'd walk down the street, sometimes I'd hear people say, "There's the kid from such and such commercial!" or "Look! There's the boy from that soft drink ad!" In those days, I got a kick out of being recognized. Since back in the day televisions had no remote controls, people had to sit through the commercials, unlike now, when we can simply switch the channel from the comfort of our sofa. This is why people started to recognize me—more and more with each commercial—and I have to admit that I liked it. Today there are moments when it is hard for me to find even a moment of peace and tranquillity to go sit in a park or play a game of pool with my friends. People recognize me, and this means I have to sacrifice certain things that for other people are normal: like eating at a restaurant, going for a walk, strolling on the beach. . . . Not because I don't want to do them, but because in doing them I don't find the peace and tranquillity I seek. And even so, I do them anyway, but I can never be anonymous. Anonymity is something I oftentimes miss, but the truth is that fame has brought me so many other blessings that I have no complaints; at the end of the day, it is a part of my work, and it is therefore something I enjoy. Most people are kind and friendly, and most of them respect my right to privacy. It always feels good to hear someone tell me that I mean something to them, whether it's because one of my songs helped them find love or because they enjoyed one of my concerts. That is all very important to me because it is the reason why I do what I do: I like giving people a little bit of joy and I enjoy myself in the process.

Fame is a curious phenomenon. When you have it, there is so much you can do with it. It is not just about people recognizing you in the street or about the photographers taking pictures of you. Fame is also a tool that, if you know how to handle it well, can serve to reach millions and millions of people to convey a message, by communicating and connecting with them. That is something I try not to forget. Of course, a lot of sacrifices must be made for the sake of fame, on both a personal and a professional level, but at the end of the day, what matters is knowing how to use it for what's truly important.

MENUDO

MY FATHER ONCE told me: "I curse the day you got into Menudo. That day I lost my son."

He was absolutely right. To a certain extent, he lost his son and I lost my father.

In those days it was hard to know what was coming. We could not even begin to imagine what lay ahead. I only saw the countless opportunities, the thousands of amazing things that still awaited me, and the great path that was opening up before me. No boy—not even when he is a grown man—can discern what will happen when his life's path is altered.

It was impossible to understand how much it was going to take for me to reach what I wanted. At that moment, all

I knew was that I longed for it with all of my being—my heart and my soul. I had worked hard with great effort and determination and I knew how far I wanted to go. Being onstage was my dream and I was willing to do whatever it took to get there. In this sense, Menudo was an obsession— it was all I could think about. Between the ages of ten and twelve, I could barely sleep just thinking about how badly I wanted it.

When it finally came, it ceased to be a dream and became my everyday reality. It was a moment that would determine the course of my life.

What it gave me was magnificent—experiences and emotions that deeply marked me and made me a better person. What it cost me was my childhood. But I gained invaluable lessons through what I learned and what I lost. And just as I would never want to lose any of the beautiful memories I have from those years, I also don't want to forget some of the troubles I endured. Difficult times gave me the ability to appreciate joyful ones, and they also helped to strengthen me as a man. It's just like everything else in life: If it weren't for the bad things in life, we would never be able to appreciate the good ones.

When I was young, my mother always said: "My son, in this life everything is possible. But you have to know how to do it." She said it because she knows me well; she knew that back then I wanted everything, and in those days everything was Menudo.

I drove my father crazy to take me to the auditions. I would plead with him: "Take me! Take me! Take me!" I would beg him in every possible way imaginable, and begged so much that I don't know how he didn't throw me off a cliff. Until finally one day he said: "All right, let's go."

I was so happy.

This was 1983. Today it is hard to understand what Menudo was at that time, but the truth is it was unlike anything else out there. I would even dare to say that to this day it remains a unique episode in the history of music. Before there were any bands like New Edition, the Backstreet Boys, New Kids on the Block, 'N Sync, or Boyz II Men, there was Menudo. It was the first Latin American boy band that reached international fame. The band was so successful that there was talk of "Menudomania" and "Menuditis," and it was often compared to the Beatles and Beatlemania.

Menudo began when the producer Edgardo Diaz formed a group of five young boys, all of them Puerto Rican. The uniqueness of Menudo, what I believe made Menudo completely distinctive—and allowed its fame to last for so long—is that the band members were always changing. The idea was that each member would only stay until he turned sixteen, and at that point he would have to retire and his place in the band would open up for a new member. This way, the boys were always young, preserving the joy and innocence of adolescence. The first Menudo was composed of two sets of brothers: the Melendezes (Carlos, Ricky, and Oscar), and the Sallaberrys (Fernando and Nefty). They released their first album in 1977, and from that moment on the group's fame grew exponentially: In just a few short years they were filling stadiums the length and width of Latin America, and their photos were plastered across the press, even in Asia. They became a world-wide phenomenon, and when RCA, the music label, got wind of what was going on, they signed them to a multi-million-dollar deal. This made them even more famous, garnering millions of young fans throughout the United States and the rest of the world. In fact, one of the most important English-language TV networks in the United States used the group's music to teach its viewers how to speak Spanish.

So when I was very little (in the late seventies, early eighties), Menudo was awesome. A worldwide phenomenon. A total hit. How could I not have wanted to be a part of that? Especially considering that the phenomenon had been born on my island? I knew all of their songs by heart—I had been singing them as long as I can remember. In fact, I loved singing so much that, with the innate confidence of youth, I felt that getting into the group was not an impossible dream. . . . So I dedicated myself to making it happen.

But like everything in life, my entrance into Menudo would not come without its fair share of contradictions. Despite the fact that the boys from Menudo were my idols and I yearned to be a part of the group, for the majority of kids my age Menudo was a girl thing. Culturally and socially, we were so conditioned—in part due to ignorance and in part to envy—to think that real men don't like to sing and dance, that for a kid like me to want to do it was considered ridiculous. In fact, when my friends from school asked me why I wanted to get into Menudo, I would always say that it was "for the girls, the money, and the travel." I should have told them the truth—that I wanted to sing and dance onstage—but I have no doubt that they would have made fun of me. Boys weren't supposed to "like" Menudo. So instead of telling the truth, I simply went along with it and said what was expected of me, choosing the path of least resistance. At that time, it was in no way a traumatic experience, but now I realize how sad it is that I didn't feel comfortable enough to tell the truth.

After pleading for months, I finally had the opportunity to audition. My father took me to the place where the auditions were being held, and I perfectly recall that on the way there I felt completely calm. Even though it would have been normal for me to be even just a little bit nervous, I was very relaxed because I knew I was going to do well and that the executives would have no option other than to choose me.

And that's how it went . . . almost. I did very well at the audition. They loved how I sang and how I danced, but there was one problem: I was too short. The rest of the boys in the group were a head and a half taller than me, and the executives wanted all the boys in the group to be more or less the same height. But instead of discouraging me, that initial rejection only served to fuel my determination. I showed up again at an audition nine months later, but once again I failed because I was still too short. At one point they even suggested that I buy a basketball and play to see if it would help me grow! Kind of cynical, right?

But, of course, I did not allow myself to become discouraged. I persisted until finally, by the third audition, I made it. I had not really grown much since the last two auditions, but for some reason this time my stature did not seem to bother them. I think it was in part because they saw how badly I wanted to get in. "Looks like you're just never going to grow!" they said.

The day of that third audition, they called me and said that they wanted to do another audition at the home of one of the band manager's assistants. I of course went to her house, where I sang a couple of songs. When I finished, she said to me, "Now, let's go to the office." I thought it was a bit strange, but since I didn't know any better, I followed her.

The surprise came when we arrived at the group's offices, and my parents were there to meet me. At first I didn't understand why they were there, until someone finally explained: "You passed the audition! You are a Menudo!" I was speechless. I was happy, of course, but at the same time I could not believe it. They congratulated me and we celebrated, but what was really unbelievable was that they told me at seven o'clock at night, and by eight o'clock the next morning I was on a plane to Orlando, where the band was based. As soon as I arrived I went straight to do interviews, meet the stylists, and get fitted for wardrobe. In less than twenty-four hours my life changed completely.

I left my family behind, along with my neighborhood, my friends, and absolutely everything that was familiar to me. It was a very abrupt change that could have been traumatic had it not been for the fact that I was on cloud nine. I was so overjoyed that I had more than enough energy to do everything I had to do. I had to learn eighteen dance routines in just ten days, and I can say that it's something I am genuinely proud of, because it took some people four days just to learn one. It was a very intense time that came with its share of challenges, but I was so happy I felt like I was on top of the world.

Just one month after I joined the group, I made my debut at the Luis A. Ferré Center for Fine Arts in San Juan, Puerto Rico. Ricky Melendez (the last standing member of the original group) was the one leaving, and as such was the one who introduced me that night, which was very special for me. It was planned that after his presentation I would sing alone in the middle of the stage, while the rest of the group remained seated on a staircase behind me. It was a spectacular moment. I was not nervous at all—in fact, quite the opposite! I grabbed the microphone and started to sing, walking from one side of the stage to the other, moving to the rhythm of the music. I was very pleased with my performance, especially when I finished and the audience gave me such a thunderous hand. It made me feel so good that I realized that this was definitely what I wanted to do from then on.

But that night I also had one of my first lessons on how things were done with Menudo. When I finished my song and left the stage, the band manager was waiting for me backstage. I was still flying high, euphoric from the applause, when he approached me, screaming: *"Did I not tell you to stand in the middle of the stage?!"*

He was right. He had said so because of the lighting, and I had completely forgotten to follow his instructions. I was going from one side of the stage to the other, when they wanted me to stay planted in one spot where they could shine the lights on me steadily. The poor guys in the lighting crew were probably losing their minds trying to follow me with the spotlights.

The mistake was such a big deal that from that moment on, never again did I move when I wasn't supposed to move. I would learn that lesson, as I would many more in the years to come. That was the discipline of Menudo: You either did things the way you were told or you were not part of the group. It was that simple.

THE GOOD LIFE

AFTER WORKING SO hard to get into the band, I was not going to do—or fail to do—anything that would cost me my place in the group. Menudo was more than a new world to me; it was another galaxy. When we traveled, we took a private jet—we're talking about a jumbo 737! In the cities where we performed, we would not just stay in a simple hotel suite, or even on a whole floor; the *entire hotel* would be reserved just for us! Sometimes there would be a whole floor just to entertain us, replete with pinball machines and video games. We lived in our very own Disney World, any child's wildest dream. It was so much fun! Every day was a new adventure, and I loved every second of it. We worked very hard, but when it was time to relax, we were treated like kings.

The other thing I always loved about Menudo was that it was like one big family. The free time we had was spent playing around and talking—and sometimes fighting—like five brothers. Since I was the youngest and the smallest in size, some of the other guys would play the role of the older brothers. When we were among the masses, when the fans would trample us with excitement, they always looked after me in the midst of the madness. And that made me feel special.

We traveled all over the world. We had concerts in Japan, the Philippines, Europe, South America, and for the first time in the history of the group, we did a tour through the United States, which included twenty-four shows at Radio City Music Hall in New York. It was crazy and impressive to see thousands and thousands of people stopping traffic on Sixth Avenue in front of Radio City and around the entire block! When we looked down from our dressing room, it was like a sea of people. Hundreds of police officers had to form a human barrier on Sixty-third Street and the corner of Lexington Avenue, where our hotel was.

Our fans were passionate, and they would stop at nothing. I remember another time we were in Argentina and there was a throng of at least five thousand girls outside the hotel. They had pins, photographs, flags, and all the Menudo paraphernalia. The girls would scream and yell out each time we would appear at the windows. All you had to do was put an arm out the window to drive them crazy. They would sing our songs along with cheers, like you would hear at soccer stadiums, but adapting them to the group. Later, some guys showed up—I guess they were upset because of all the attention Menudo was getting from the girls—and they started to sing their own cheers, but insulting us and calling us names. Suddenly one of the boys went to where the girls were and tried to take down the Puerto Rican flag. . . . Well, the girls fought back hard!

They beat him up so badly that I think he barely made it out alive.

Things like that happened to us all the time. It was truly crazy.

What a change! Before I became a part of the group, my life was completely different. From a simple life in Puerto Rico, where I lived surrounded by family and friends, and hardly ever wandered beyond the few square blocks of my neighborhood, I leaped into a world of fame, luxury, and worship. I went from being the beloved son of my parents and adored grandson of my grandparents to being an international star who traveled the world giving concerts on some of the most important stages on the planet. Naturally, there were moments when I felt lost and would have liked to have my mother or father around to comfort me. During the whole time I was in Menudo, they were always concerned about me and we talked very often, but of course, that was not always enough. I remember, for example, once when we were on tour in Brazil, I called my mother one night and said, "Mami, I can't take it anymore. I'm so exhausted, I want to come home."

She consoled me however she could and said: "My son, if this is what you want, don't worry. Tomorrow we will talk to the lawyers and arrange everything so that you can come home." But right away she added: "Right now it is too late at night to do it, but if this is what you want, I will call the lawyer first thing in the morning."

After speaking to her I calmed down and was able to fall asleep and get some much-needed rest. In fact, by the following morning I had completely forgotten about what was bothering me the day before. I called my mother very early the next day and said: "Mami, I'm fine now! Don't worry. Don't call the lawyers. Everything is fine."

My mother's attitude was what made me feel so much better. If I had decided to leave Menudo at that moment, things would have been pretty complicated. I would have probably gotten sued for breach of contract, and the news would have exploded in the media. People would have asked me all sorts of questions and rumors would have started as to why a band member was leaving the group when everything seemed to be going so great. . . . I realize now that it would have been a huge deal. But no matter the consequences, my mother was willing to deal with the whole thing. All she wanted was for me to stop sounding as upset as I sounded over the phone.

And so I forged ahead. Just like every other person who has to wake up in the morning and go to work, of course I had my moments of weakness and anxiety, but the euphoria that was always going on around me kept pushing me forward. I knew I was living through something extraordinary, and as tired as I may have been sometimes, I didn't want to miss a thing.

CONNECTING WITH OTHER KIDS

IT WAS THANKS to all the hard work I was doing that I had the opportunity to have so many amazing experiences and meet so many amazing people, a connection I felt with even more clarity when, for example, we became UNICEF ambassadors. The band managers wanted to make the most of our trips around the world, so in our roles as ambassadors we would invite underprivileged children—who lived a reality that was very different from ours—to our shows. Many times they were orphans, or homeless children living on the street who had faced intense hardship in their lives at a very young age.

In those days, I think our smallest concert was for an audience of about 70,000 people. We also had the world record of 200,000 people in attendance for our concert in the Morumbi Stadium in São Paulo. But when it came to spending time with these children and bringing a little bit of joy into their lives, all the glamour of the private jets, having entire hotels to ourselves, private chefs, personal bodyguards, tutors, assistants, and so on—all of this ceased to exist. The organizers would say to us, "Hold on for a second; now we are going to spend time with children who are no more or no less than you. They simply live a very different reality than yours." And the chance to be able to spend time with those children was one of the most valuable experiences that Menudo ever gave me. I learned to see life from another perspective, to comprehend what is truly meaningful and what is not—a lesson that is beyond important for an adolescent living in the world of luxury and abundance.

I truly began to understand how many children live in other parts of the world. It was not easy, and may have been a heavy hit of reality, but I loved the experience. It was very special because I was the youngest of the group— at that time I was twelve—and the boy ahead of me was fourteen. There is a big difference between twelve and fourteen, and almost all the kids they invited were my age or even younger, so I was quickly establishing a special connection with them. They had such a different sense of wisdom than my own, and I can say I learned so much from them.

I didn't feel bad about having so many more material possessions in comparison to the little they had. I felt good because of what I was able to share with them! But I also started to realize that although I had many things they didn't have, they possessed so many other things that I was missing—for example, freedom. Everything is relative in this life, and what is normal for you may be a treasure for someone else. Although they were lacking possessions, they had the freedom to go wherever they wanted whenever they chose. And even though I loved the stage, and the fans' endless admiration, the life I led was very strict. For us, a typical day began with school lessons at eight in the morning, and then we'd autograph records before lunch. In the afternoons we would have photo shoots, rehearsals, and media interviews. These children, on the other hand, did whatever they wanted, as life on the streets gave them absolute freedom. Granted, that liberty comes with a great deal of hardship, but back then I couldn't help but notice how I had to ask for permission to go around the corner, and they could do whatever they wanted without checking with anybody. We were being watched at every moment and there was a series of rules we had to follow for security. So even though I had such a wonderful life, unique and joyful, I undoubtedly also found great beauty in their absolute freedom.

I don't know if I realized then the impact these experiences were going to have on my life in the long run. I don't think that at that moment I thought, "This experience is going to affect my life forever." I believe it wasn't until years later that I realized how deeply the time spent with those kids affected me, as these experiences planted the seed for the philanthropic work I began to do later and continue to do to this very day.

LESSONS LEARNED

THE YEARS I spent with Menudo were a time of many changes and many lessons learned. First, because Menudo *was* my adolescence, a very important phase in the evolution of any child. But it was also important because of the sense of discipline it instilled in me and the professional growth I experienced. What I learned there undoubtedly created the foundation for everything that came afterward. I never would have arrived at where I am today had it not been for everything I saw and learned with Menudo.

Now, as I write these pages, I see that I had a very intense and unusual adolescence, but I can guarantee that back then everything seemed to flow quite naturally. In the midst of this chaos, I never ceased to be a young boy with needs, curiosities, fears, and the questioning that is normal for any boy that age. Somehow or other I had to become a man under the hot lights of the stage, far away from my parents, and in the gaze of thousands and thousands of people. We were boys of only fourteen, fifteen, and sixteen years, and we had about 250,000 girls throwing themselves at us. Was I ready to fill this role? Although back then I would have said yes, I later found out that I was far from being ready.

When I got to Menudo, I didn't know anything about sex, which to a certain extent was perfectly normal, given that I was just twelve years old. But more than anything, in my house sex was never something we would discuss. Incredible, isn't it? Today I find it very funny. My father is a very handsome man—a man who has lived and had his fair share of romances and today has a beautiful woman by his side. I am sure he could have taught me a thing or two about sex. But with all of that—be it because of modesty or shyness—in my house that was not a subject that was ever touched on.

He probably thought I was too young back then to have this information, which I understand, but the truth is that sexuality was a subject that was already coming at me from all angles, be it from television, conversations with friends at school, or older cousins and siblings. Today, children are that much more exposed to this type of content than the generations of the past. With the Internet, just the tap of a key can bring you into a world you had never imagined. That's why it's important to know that when your son comes to you with a question like the one I came to my father with back then, it is almost guaranteed that he already knows the answer: What he wants to see is how *you* are going to answer it. The child is testing the waters to see how cool you are. This is why I think it is crucial to speak to your children openly, so it is you who gives them the information they seek and not some total stranger.

In my family, communication has always been very open. I have always had great communication with my mother, and nowadays my communication with my dad is exemplary. But sex was just not something we could talk about back then. My father is an incredible human being. He is a professional psychologist and he has a very particular way of looking at the world, very open. Everyone loves him. For many years he worked with institutionalized people in Puerto Rico, and God knows what kinds of stories he must have heard. But I am convinced that it is because of these experiences and because of his special soul that he is so kind to the people around him. He has always been a person who has dedicated himself to his family, and my relationship with him today is a testament to all that he gave me and continues to give me. I am thirty-eight years old; my father is sixty-one; and even though we were not together for a large part of my adolescence, we have made up for lost time and today we are very close.

Anyway, even though I was a big star back then because of Menudo, I was a late bloomer. Many of my friends had already played the role of heartbreakers and had even been with girls. All of them, actually, except for me. In other words, of all my friends I was the only virgin, and I received constant pressure from them. They would ask me over and over again: "When is it going to happen? When are you going to be ready?" Until the day finally arrived when I had sex with a girl. She was nice, but my decision had a lot more to do with the pressure I felt from my friends, as well as simply the pressure in our society that says a man is never supposed to say no if he is given the opportunity to have sex—even more so since I was a part of Menudo, and there was an unspoken understanding that the most successful of us was the one who got the most girls. I knew I had to fulfill this duty, but I felt uncomfortable and could not enjoy this moment that according to my expectations was meant to be more romantic, with perhaps a bit more fireworks.

She was a pretty girl and I liked her, but the truth is that there was no sense of closeness or intimacy between us, and that's why I don't think it was such a special experience. I remember I was left with a "That's it?" kind of a feeling, and thought, "This is what everyone was talking about? Ugh, this is awful!" Obviously, it wasn't the girl's fault; it had to do with the circumstances at hand. I found the whole scenario uncomfortable and even a bit funny. I am sure there are many more people, be they gay or straight, who can identify with their first time not being so special . . . and how could it be, when we have no idea what we are doing? It goes without saying that later on I encountered women with whom I felt things and had an amazing connection, and when I discovered the intense sensation that can be shared by a man and woman during sex, I was able to be with more women and take pleasure in their company.

THE END OF AN ERA

MENUDO, IN THE meantime, continued to release albums and go on tour. Even though superficially the group and I seemed to be doing well, on the inside both of us had problems. By 1987, the group's album sales were starting to fall and we had to switch record labels. Eventually, these problems made us have to change our image completely. Our costumes and hairstyles became more "rock" and our music changed as well: We left pop music behind to dedicate ourselves to a harder genre. We released the album *Somos los Hijos del Rock* in Spanish, and for the fans in the Philippines we did a version entitled *In Action*, which had songs in English and Tagalog. Shortly after, we released an album in English called *Sons of Rock*, which resulted in another hit, called "You Got Potential." The success led us on a forty-city tour throughout the United States. It was a very exciting phase because we were able to reinvent ourselves to reach our fans through a different kind of music.

What did not change during those years was our way of working. Of the many things I learned in Menudo, the discipline is what has had the greatest impact on my career and character. We never said no. It did not matter what they asked of us; the response was always positive. We would say, "Yes, let's do it!" and we would take off to wherever for whatever—a promotional appearance, a radio station interview, signing autographs for fans at a record store, rehearsing—we would always jump at the opportunity. Many times we would do all these things on the same day. We would start at dawn on a radio station; we would run to photo shoots with the press, from there to the record store, and later to a hospital for a charitable appearance, and then to the rehearsal and sound check for that night's show. It was exhausting. Many times we would work for fourteen hours, five or six days straight, and on the seventh day we would get on a plane or bus to head to another city.

I worked so intensely when I was in Menudo that by the last year I was already fed up with being in the band. I still loved the performances, the music, and being onstage; but to be completely honest, I was simply exhausted. I just couldn't take it anymore. The band manager asked me to stay for one more year because some of the other boys were leaving the group at the time, and even though it was something I really didn't feel like doing, I said yes. My original contract with the band was for three years, but I had already spent four years with them. That last year made it five years total.

The truth is, I only stayed because I had a lot of respect and love for both the band and the crew. Obviously, after spending years on the road together, we had become a family. Besides the professional relationship we developed, we also had a lot of care for one another, and I did not want to leave them hanging at a moment when they needed me. So I stayed for one more year, but on my own terms, which I insisted on, and which they were willing to accept. When I began with Menudo, there were only two of us in the group who spoke English. So the other boy and I were the ones called on every time we had to do an interview in English, and in the meantime the other boys were allowed to stay in the hotel room, relaxing and watching TV. That didn't seem fair to me. I wanted to rest and watch television, too! So for my last year with Menudo, I asked the manager to assign that job to someone else. Basically, all I wanted to do were the shows. Fortunately, they accepted my conditions and that's how we did it.

It was not arrogance on my part, nor did I want to be difficult. I just really wanted to leave the group. Aside from being tired of the grind, while the rest of the guys gave themselves the good life with sports cars, motorcycles, and everything else, I was receiving a salary of just $400 a month. The reason is that when I joined the group, my parents and their lawyers decided, in order to prevent any misunderstandings, to put my money into a trust from which I could only withdraw $400 monthly; everything else would stay frozen in the account until I turned eighteen. It made me furious that they gave me so little money when I was working so hard. I know there are a lot of people who work a lot harder than I did and earned less than what I got in those days, but you have to understand that I was a young boy and my point of reference was the other members of Menudo. So I felt I did not have anything, and it made me angry.

In my mind there were plenty of reasons to want a change in my life. I was tired of the pace, I was tired of not having money, but more than anything I felt I needed a new challenge. The years spent with Menudo had changed me in so many ways: I was on the brink of adulthood and all I really wanted now was to have a chance to think—to really think—about who I wanted to be and what I wanted to make of my life.

So, in July of 1989 I left Menudo. My last concert with the band was in the Luis A. Ferré Center for the Arts in San Juan. It was the perfect venue for me to finish my career with the group, since that is where I had debuted with them. It was finally time to close the chapter and move on.

After the show, I returned home without a clue as to what I was going to do with my life. Yes, I had to finish high school, but as far as my career went, my future remained uncertain. For the time being, I needed to reconnect with my family and relearn how to live with them again. This is a difficult task for any teenager, but I think the circumstances made my adaptation even more difficult. It had been five years since I had last lived with them, and the experiences I had lived through had nothing to do with the life I had at home with my family. I felt disconnected, lonely, and even a bit lost.

Many people believe that the song that best describes me is "Livin' La Vida Loca," but really they are mistaken. The one that comes closest to describing my life is a song written for me by the great artist and composer Ricardo Arjona, entitled *"Asignatura Pendiente"* ("Pending Assignment"). The lyrics brilliantly capture the day in 1984 when I left Puerto Rico for the first time. *From your tiny hand waving good-bye / That rainy afternoon in San Juan / With the kisses that I carry with me.* Without knowing it, the day I left Puerto Rico I was leaving behind those who loved me; I was leaving my childhood behind. I looked forward and saw only blue skies and a massive universe open to all possibilities. Now that I was back at home, that same sky looked gray and confused, and the many possibilities that before had looked open to me were now dissipating into the horizon.

The lyrics of Arjona's song reflect the challenge and wonder of success. Success is a double-edged sword, because for everything that one does, something else is sacrificed; for every road taken, another one is left uncharted. It is the law of life. I chose the stage, being in front of an audience, hearing the applause and feeling the adulation. It is a feeling that fulfills me and brings me great joy. But now, at this age, I know that the love of my fans sometimes is not unconditional. The warmth of their love may be wonderful, but the intensity of fame can sometimes burn.

In my culture, we have a saying: *No hay mal que por bien no venga* (which loosely means "Everything happens for a reason"). We should instead have an expression that says, "Today, I choose the path that has always been mine." To say that leaving Puerto Rico on that day was a mistake is to forget all the wonderful things that came afterward, all the extraordinary things I would have missed out on had I not left home. I don't think that leaving Puerto Rico, or having spent time in Menudo, was all good or all bad. It was both. I had to do what I did to be where I am today.

We all grow up at our own pace. While there are people who have the good fortune to grow up with the guidance, counsel, and care of their parents, other people have to adapt to circumstances and become adults very early on in life. For better or worse, this was the case for me. At the ripe old age of twelve, an opportunity came my way that would change my life completely: Menudo. It was one of the most successful bands in history, and becoming a part of it was a dream come true, everything I had always wanted. But like all great things in life, the experience did not come without a great deal of sacrifice. I had to leave behind my family, my school, and my friends—everything that I knew. I sacrificed my youth and my innocence, and even though today I know I will never be able to recover these things, I can wholeheartedly say that I have no regrets. It was very difficult, but that's what becoming a man is all about: confronting the challenges that life throws our way, and learning to grow with them.

But when I first returned home, I still did not see how my new experiences had changed me, and I did not realize how much more I still needed to grow. On many levels, I was already very much a man—I had lived, traveled, and had my experiences—but back then I did not see the spiritual path I would need to walk in order to connect with who I really am. During the time I was in Menudo I learned a lot and matured at an alarming rate. Not only did I learn to sing, dance, and everything you need to have a career in show business. I also started to experience the world on my own, far from the protective gaze of my parents. That said, I did miss out on some of the essential things in life, and all of the uncertainty, fear, and confusion of adolescence did not take long to hit me hard when I returned home. It wasn't until I returned home to my family and the island I had left behind that I noticed the feeling of emptiness inside me. Like many, back then I believed happiness was something I could find outside me, and not within.

TWO

MEETING DESTINY

BACK WHEN I USED TO DRIVE MY FATHER CRAZY ABOUT how much I wanted to join Menudo, I remember feeling that if I made it into the group I would never have to worry about anything ever again. I would earn money, I would live with the other four guys, who in those days were my idols, and all of my dreams would come true. I thought that if only I could get into the band, my life would be made because *I knew* in the deepest part of myself that I wanted to be an artist. Nothing was going to stop me from achieving my dream. What I didn't know was that the shortest distance between two points is not always a straight line, and to achieve my goals there was still a lot of work to do.

In Menudo, everything was more or less routine and predictable, and the only thing I had to do was follow a series of rules that were given to me. But after I left the band, my career stopped being a straight line and turned into a series of points that might, at first glance, seem haphazardly dispersed. Instead of focusing on continuing to be a musician, I dabbled in a bit of everything, because these were the opportunities that came my way. That's how I ended up working in film, theater, and television before I came back to music. If it hadn't been for the variety of those experiences, I wouldn't have been able to open up to the destiny that awaited me. Today I ask myself if this was about destiny at all, or if I myself was somehow creating it through the great power of consciousness.

FINDING MYSELF AT HOME

WHEN I RETURNED to Puerto Rico after five years with the band, I felt totally lost; it was almost like I didn't know who I really was. Part of me wanted to distance myself from the entertainment world, but during the time I spent with Menudo, show business had become such a profound part of my existence that it would have been like removing a major organ.

A lot of my unease probably had to do with the fact that I was seventeen years old, and like most boys my age, I felt I was at a crossroads in my life. I was faced with a series of grown-up decisions, but I was facing them with the mind of a child. Ironically, while the time in Menudo forced me to grow up and learn things at a much faster pace than normal, on many levels I was still a child. From age twelve to seventeen I never had to make a decision for myself (my clothes, hairstyles, music, and itinerary were all decided by someone else), and that is how I functioned: doing what was expected of me, always trying to please everyone else. So when I took control of my own life, I felt completely lost: I did not know where to look or what to do. Emotionally, I was starting to feel I wasn't grounded, and I was confused. After my first experience with a girl I also shared some experiences with men, and though I did not want to confront it, my sexuality was something I was very much aware of. Inside, I felt that I was battling contradicting emotions, but the terror I felt in the face of discovering—never mind admitting—my homosexuality was such that I didn't even give myself the time to seriously stop and analyze what I was feeling. Culturally, I had always been taught that love and attraction between two men was a sin, so instead of facing what I felt, I buried it because it scared me.

Another issue when I returned to the island was that I had to face the chaos in my family. Before Menudo, my parents' divorce had never affected me. Despite the fact that they lived separately, I had a very happy childhood. Their separation was never a source of pain for me, as they always made an effort to maintain a certain balance, which gave me peace and tranquillity. But when I got into Menudo, I felt the pain for the first time. The fact that I separated from my family at such a young age had a profound impact on my family. The divorce that until then had not affected me suddenly began to affect me. While I was enjoying being part of one of the most recognized bands on the planet, traveling around the world with screaming fans everywhere, my parents began fighting more than ever. Their relationship, which had until now been harmonious, became irreconcilable; and I was stuck in the middle of the storm.

On the one hand, my return home meant I would get a break from the pressures of the group, the promotional tours, and the constant stress of work. On the other hand, it was hard for me to face all the anger and resentment that had built up in my absence. And I am not just talking about the anger between my parents; I am also referring to the resentment I had toward them for putting me right in the middle of their battle. Because of their conflict, I was forced to take sides—which is something no child should ever have to do. Every visit to Puerto Rico was a nightmare. It was ridiculous and also very painful. Deep down inside me I began to develop a profound spite toward both of them because they were forcing me to choose between the two people in the world I loved most. When you're young, the concept of God is taught to you by your parents. But as you try to understand the abstract concept of "superior being," the ones who play that role in your day-to-day life are your mother and father. When Mom and Dad (or God, as it were) make mistakes that end up hurting you, you have no idea how to forgive them. What seems crazy is that I grew up in a religion where I was the one who had to apologize to God for my mistakes, but here it was God, aka Mom and Dad, hurting me by making me choose between them.

There are many children in the world who go through this type of situation, and it breaks my heart to see that parents don't realize the damage they are doing to their kids. Even though my parents had their reasons for fighting, all I could think was, "Why do their issues have to affect me?" I worked like crazy and I couldn't even enjoy my time off like the rest of the guys in the group.

With time, I have come to realize that I killed myself

working so hard in Menudo because a part of me wanted to forget about the problems that awaited me back in Puerto Rico. While I was working and traveling the world, I felt safe and distanced from the reality of what was going on in my family. I didn't know how to handle the situation, so I simply endured it for only a few days at a time—at most—always wanting to get back to work as soon as possible.

But now that I was going to be home for the foreseeable future, there was no escape: I had to face my reality, no matter what. For a long time I couldn't understand why they fought and were so angry at each other all the time, but what I realize today is that they were doing the best they could under their circumstances, and seeing it this way has helped me forgive them.

It took time, but I finally understood that if they were fighting it was only because they both wanted the best for me. My parents each had their own point of view, and though their stubbornness may have caused me a lot of pain, they were doing it for the most important reason: because they loved me and I was their son. And what can be better than that? There are parents who abandon their children and don't protect them. My parents were never like that. It was the total opposite: They always worried about me and they adored me to no end. When I finally understood this, I was able to find peace. In my heart, I forgave all of the pain and anger they caused me, and today we have one of the most loving and caring relationships possible. I treasure every moment they spend with my children and me, and I try to see them as often as possible.

COMING OF AGE

ONE OF THE things that I did love about my return to Puerto Rico was that all I had to do was focus on being a teenager, and it was a huge relief. I finished high school, and with my small allowance I was even able to buy a car, which I would use to go from party to party and stay out until the crack of dawn.

But for as busy as I appeared to the outside world at the time—between spending time with my family and friends, going to parties, studying, and so on—inside I felt completely lost. I was exhausted and confused and didn't know where I stood. Although I think it's normal to feel that way at that age, I am sure the experience with Menudo had only intensified my doubts. I had enjoyed my years in the group immensely, but when it was all over I didn't know if I wanted to continue in the music business. The stage that once drew me in now caused me mixed emotions, and I simply had no idea which path to take. I needed time to think.

I finished my studies, and on December 24, 1989, I celebrated my eighteenth birthday; with the arrival of that day, aside from becoming an adult, I gained financial independence: I could finally access the bank accounts that had been frozen for years, and do whatever I chose with the money I had earned. And to celebrate, I decided I was going to live it up! Thirteen days after my birthday, on January 6, 1990, I moved to New York City.

The original plan was to go for only one week—or at least that's what I told everyone. I took my pillow and my backpack and just a few clothes, so no one would be suspicious or guess my intentions. But the moment I landed at JFK, I called my mother and said: "Mami, I'm staying in New York."

"What? Oh, no!" she replied. "How can you stay in New York? Why don't you go to Miami instead?"

I think it made her nervous for me to live in such a large city, because she was afraid I'd get mugged, or who knows what else. "Come on, Mami," I said to her, "you've watched too many movies. Don't worry. I've made up my mind and I decided that I want to live here for a while."

Like I said, I needed time to think, but I also think I needed to take it down a notch when it came to partying. During those six months I spent in Puerto Rico, there was a lot of craziness and many adventures. I had a blast, but inside I knew I was avoiding the great question that followed me: What was I going to do next? And so when I arrived in New York, the last thing I wanted to do was party. To the contrary: I wanted to find peace and tranquillity. I had a couple of good friends who were newlyweds and had also just moved to New York, and they put me up in their house for a little while. During my stay with them, I got to know the city and had some time to settle into my new home.

I found a small but comfortable place in Long Island City, in a Greek neighborhood, just down the street from my friends. After Menudo, where I had had access to such unbelievable luxuries—our own private jet, five-star hotels, incredible dinners—all I wanted was a simple life. Of course, I could have found an apartment in Manhattan close to all the best restaurants and in the most happening neighborhood, but that's not what I was looking for at the time. In my apartment in Queens I lived a simple life, with the basic necessities. For the first time in my life I could live exactly as *I* pleased, without the pressure of my parents, my manager, my producer, or anyone else telling me what to do. I did what I wanted, when I wanted, and how I wanted. And if I did not feel like doing anything, I did absolutely *nothing at all*.

On the weekends I would go into Manhattan to a record store, where I would do paid "meet and greets" and they would have me sign records, buttons, and all types of Menudo paraphernalia. This was perfect for me because it was just a few hours of work per week and provided me with an income. On the weekends, friends who were studying in Boston usually came to visit. Almost every day I would go to bed at dawn, but not because I was out at some party. In fact, when you are eighteen there is not much you can do in New York, because you cannot get into bars or clubs until you're twenty-one. My friends— who unlike me came with the desire to party—would invite me to go out with them, but I would always tell them I'd meet up with them later. I would stay at home, relaxing, and I spent hours watching movies, walking, painting. In fact, if I remember correctly, my paintings from that time were a bit melancholic. All this free time was giving me the space I needed to think, reflect, and mature. I wanted to take full advantage of this time, and have time to get to know myself.

From the time I was twelve until the time I was seventeen—the five formative years of adolescence—all I heard was: "Wear this. Cut your hair like this. Sing this. Learn this dance routine. Talk to this journalist." I never had the chance to make my own decisions, which is why I had no idea how to make them! During those same five years, I was trained—I was indoctrinated—to personify a concept. I was forced to hide my feelings and my personality at all costs. I couldn't be Kiki or Ricky. . . . The only thing that mattered was that I was a good Menudo!

While I was in New York I had a lot of time to think, and I realized that over the previous several years I had become an expert at hiding my emotions. I'd say to myself, "No, I don't want to feel this," and I would shut down. It was hard for me to say, "I love you," because the thing I feared most was rejection. I had spent so much time thinking that the only thing that mattered was that you follow a certain set of rules for other people to like you, so I didn't have a clue what it meant to be genuine and express my own feelings.

For nine months, I lived happily among the people in the great city of New York, and experienced what it was like to live like "a normal person" instead of a celebrity. It wasn't the life of a monk or an ascetic, but I created a peaceful and relaxed lifestyle for myself, and that's the way I continued to live my life from then on. I would sit on a park bench and look at the people passing by, without being accosted for autographs or photographs. In this city of millions, I was anonymous. And that simple life, enjoying and noticing simple things like the change of seasons, allowed me to find the inner peace that I had lost. I reconnected with the dreams and fantasies of my youth, and I still believed in making all my dreams come true.

The silence allowed me to think of the future and genuinely ask myself what I really wanted to do. One possibility was to study acting at New York University, but I didn't know if I wanted to go back to the stage. Show business was still a source of mixed emotions, and one day I told my mother I wanted to study computer science. She, of course, immediately said, "Son, please don't do that."

I felt angry that she was not going to support what I wanted to do, so I responded: "Mami, I'm telling you that I want to study, which is what all moms want for their kids. And you are telling me you don't want me to? How is that possible?"

"Son," she said, "you may not realize it yet, but it's your destiny to be onstage." She already knew what I was about even before I was willing to accept the truth.

"Mami, don't even think about that!" I said to her. "I never want to go back to the stage. I've had enough."

I was a bit annoyed, so we didn't touch upon the subject again. A few months later she came to visit me and we went to see a concert at Radio City. Suddenly, in the middle of the show, I turned to say something to her, only to find her with tears streaming down her face. She was sobbing like a baby.

"Mami, what's wrong?" I asked, worried.

"Son, you just can't give up on show business," she said. "That is your place, in center stage, in the spotlight."

My mother's words stayed in my head. They affected me, of course, but not enough to make me change my mind. Now that I think about it, I never really sought out the stage. It was the stage that found me. I did it because the opportunity came quite naturally. Like everything else in my life, it was as if destiny itself had laid it out before me, and the only thing I had to do was decide whether to take advantage of the opportunity. Now more than ever, after everything I have been through, I am convinced that this is how everything in life is, that this is its magic and its beauty. We all walk down a karmic path, a spiritual journey, and we each have the opportunity to decide what to do with our own lives. It is as if we are wandering through the desert and all of a sudden a horse appears. We can ignore it and keep walking, or we can get on that horse. And if we do mount it, we can just sit there and do nothing and let the horse drive us, or we can take control of the reins and gallop toward the place where we truly want to go. When an opportunity comes my way, I am the only one who decides to either take it or leave it.

Around that time, one of the opportunities that came my way arrived by telephone. I called a former colleague of mine in Mexico just to say hello and see how he was doing. While we were talking he invited me to spend a few days in Mexico City with him, and, since I had all the time in the world, I accepted the invitation without thinking twice. A few days later I boarded a flight toward another great city. The original idea was that I'd stay for just one week, but, just like when I arrived in New York, my plans changed drastically. . . .

A few nights after I arrived, I went to the theater to see a play that was produced by and featured three close friends, who happened to be great stars of the Mexican stage: Angelica Ortiz, Angelica Maria, and Angelica Vale. The play was called *Mamá Ama el Rock (Mama Loves Rock)*, a musical comedy. Besides the fact that I was excited to see my friends, I've always loved going to the theater and I never missed an opportunity to see a new show. It had been a long time since I'd seen these friends, so when we started talking they asked me what I was doing in New York.

"I'm studying," I answered.

What a lie! I simply didn't want to get into the details.

"Okay, forget about school," one of them replied. "You have to stay here." Her assertiveness surprised me, and right away she added, "See that guy standing over there?" She pointed to one of the actors. "He is leaving in a week and I don't know what to do. Do you want to replace him?"

Without thinking twice, I said yes, and that is how I started out in the theater world.

REACHING FOR A STAR

MY FAMILY AND my friends in New York could not believe it when I told them I was moving to Mexico, but they were all very happy for me. They knew it would be good for me to go back to work. And just like that, out of nowhere, I had to go back to being extremely intense and focused on my work. I had just one week to prepare for my theatrical debut. Yes, in one week I learned the choreography, the lines, the blocking, everything. I was back to being the disciplined soldier of my Menudo days, but I enjoyed it so much because it brought back the euphoria I had not felt for a whole year. It was crazy to dive into doing something that was totally new for me, but the truth is that the experience with Menudo had taught me how to work at a fast pace and keep up with all the hard work. And as the saying goes, *De los cobardes no se escrito nada* (Nothing has been written about cowards), so I let go of any fears I might have had and plunged headfirst into this opportunity that life had thrown my way.

I adapted to life in Mexico very naturally, with no major difficulties. Not only did I already have friends and professional connections. I also had the good fortune of moving in at first with another old work colleague. His parents and sister took me in as one more member of the family, and thanks to that I never felt alone. I loved living with them, but after a few months, when I was a bit more settled, I felt it was time to become more independent and I rented my own apartment.

There's a tradition in Mexican theater: Whenever a show reached its hundredth performance (or two hundredth, or three, or four, successively), some famous actor, director, or producer would come onstage and present the cast with a plaque to recognize the achievement.

When I began to work on *Mamá Ama el Rock* I wasn't aware of this tradition, and I didn't have a clue what a big deal it was. So when our time came to receive the award I just decided to focus on doing the best show possible. The rest of the actors, however, were extremely nervous, because they knew someone important was sitting in the audience that night. They all wanted to put on the best show in history, and when the curtain went up, the tension was palpable.

I, however, went on like normal, completely calm. I played my role as best I could, and I went home to bed. Had I known that a famous producer was watching us that night, I would have probably been just as nervous as everyone else. But since I had no idea, I was totally calm. The next day the producer called me and said he wanted to meet me personally. We spoke for a while and he ended up offering me a role on a famous soap opera called *Alcanzar una estrella (Reaching for a Star)*. I accepted, and that's how this new chapter of my life began: soap operas. The soap had great success, not only in Mexico but also all over the world, its achievement not unlike the hit shows *High School Musical* or *Glee*, which years later took off in the United States.

I ended up joining the cast in the second season, which was called *Alcanzar una estrella II (Reaching for a Star II)*. The story was set around six young boys who were in a band called Muñecos de Papel (Paper Dolls). I had the role of Pablo Loredo, one of the members of the group. The soap was so successful that later a film was made, called *Más que alcanzar una estrella (Beyond Reaching for a Star)*, in which I also had a starring role. Eventually, the show producers organized a tour for Muñecos de Papel. Needless to say, this was a complete Menudo flashback for me—although this one was not as intense, not even close— and I have to admit that I was not terribly enthusiastic about the prospect of going on tour; all I wanted to do was act. I had toured enough already! But I finally accepted and even enjoyed it because we were a great group of people who all really got along so well.

Amazingly enough, thanks to my role in the film, that year I received the Premio El Heraldo—which is the Mexican equivalent of the Oscar—for my performance. It was a great honor for me, and to this day it is one of my most treasured awards of my career.

Now that I think about it, I realize that everything I did during that time—even when I was acting—had to do with music. It was almost inevitable. And though it's tempting to say that it was all a big coincidence and it did not necessarily have to work out this way, it could also be that the universe was conspiring to move me in the right direction. Menudo was an incredible experience that taught me a lot about the music business, and even more so about myself. But the work was so intense that it left me questioning my passion. I think that deep down I never wanted to stop singing, but I had somehow buried this desire deep inside me. During the time I spent in New York, I honestly believed that I did not want to set foot on the stage again, but I think it was just because I was burned out. The effort had been so monumental, and my life during that time had been so crazy, that I just didn't see how I could continue at that pace. But the opportunities that came my way in Mexico gradually changed my point of view, and I realized that life onstage didn't always have to be as intense as it was with Menudo. In some magical way, acting reinvigorated my passion for singing, and though I enjoyed acting very much, I felt the desire and the need to sincerely express myself through music.

Needless to say, we all have to make the best of the opportunities that come our way, but we should never forget about our true passion. If in the deepest part of yourself you feel that you are a poet, regardless of whether you are a doctor or an accountant, you shouldn't stop writing your poetry. On the contrary: It is important to remember that what you do and what you are are not always the same thing. Both are part of life, part of the same journey. If you don't try to do what you are really passionate about, you will never make your dreams come true. You may have lots of things, like beautiful houses or fancy cars. You may find love and have a family that adores you. You can have all that and a lot more. But if you are a poet, and you don't write poems, how will you win the award for poetry that you have always dreamed of? If you don't cultivate your passion, you will always feel a void. You will always feel that something is missing. I am not saying that you have to leave your work and write poems twenty-four hours a day, but each and every one of us should always try as hard as possible to never abandon our dreams.

From a young age, I knew that music filled my soul immensely. I also love the connection that emerges with the audience when I perform live. The energy that comes from the crowd, with everyone moving to the rhythm of my music, is incredible. It's electric! There is nothing like it, and nothing else comes close to it. I like the work I do in film and television, but it lacks the immediate reaction and intensity of a live audience because you are on a screen. No matter what people say, to me there is nothing more amazing than the connection forged with the crowd during a live performance. I want—no, I need—that immediate reaction. The applause and the energy of the public are my addiction—they are my vice.

And that is how—through a series of haphazard chances—I returned to music. I will always be infinitely grateful to Mexico for everything it gave me, and all the opportunities it offered. It was my springboard into the rest of the world, because from theater I moved on to television soap operas, and from soaps to film, and through film I came back to music. One never knows how destiny will rear its head, and sometimes it is not in the most obvious way. Thanks to the soap opera and the film, someone at Sony Music noticed me and offered me my first solo recording contract. Obviously, I was ecstatic. The idea of making a record that would be just mine, on which I could freely express myself as I wanted, was my dream come true.

The Sony Music executive who offered me the deal handed me the contract and said: "Ricky, you have to sign this right away. If you don't sign this document before I get on a plane to Madrid tonight, I'm getting fired."

I laughed inside, and said to myself: "What a son of a bitch."

It goes without saying that today I would have waited for my attorneys to review it. But because then I was an eighteen-year-old boy and all I wanted to do was sing, I closed my eyes, signed the contract, and said to myself: "Regardless of what may happen, I want to make this album, so what difference does it make?" All I wanted was to start recording as soon as possible. I was so excited about getting back into the music world that I didn't care what the conditions were.

It was a mistake—a huge mistake. That record executive—and he will surely recognize himself when he reads this—took advantage of my ignorance and gave me a deal that offered me something like one cent of royalties for every record sold. Robbery! Today I think about it and I have to laugh at how absurd it was. But aside from this minor contractual detail, the album was the start of something phenomenal for me—something that I had been preparing for my entire life. I'd known I wanted to be an artist since I was six years old, because when I took hold of that spoon and sang for my aunts and uncles, I felt in my soul that it was the right thing to do. All of the hard work and passion I had exerted was finally now starting to come to fruition, and music came back to my life powerfully and definitively.

Of course, it would have been great if the Sony Music executive had appeared at the exact time I finished shooting the film. But such is life, and things never happen exactly when we want them to; things always seem to happen all at once! This can significantly complicate things, but I honestly believe that if we sit around waiting for opportunities to show up at the perfect moment, we'll never get anywhere in life. Life is complex, and that is how we've got to face it. That's how *Ricky Martin*, my first solo album, was recorded while I was still filming episodes of *Alcanzar a una estrella II*. I was working around the clock—but I was incredibly excited about everything that lay ahead. The day to day was challenging, but if I'd learned anything during my time in New York, it was that I could never lose sight of my big-picture goals. Thanks to the time I had given myself to think and rest, I was ready the day that destiny came knocking on my door. Deep inside I was finally sure of what I wanted to do: I wanted to be onstage.

The album was released in 1991, shortly after I returned from my tour with Muñecos de Papel. It was a huge suc-cess. One of the singles that appeared on that album was *"Fuego Contra Fuego"* ("Fire versus Fire"), for which I received gold records in Mexico, Argentina, Puerto Rico, and the United States. Receiving an award (never mind many of them) is a very exciting accomplishment, but what I loved most about that record was that it gave me the chance to get back onstage and do a tour through Latin America, where once again I came face-to-face with my audience. I was performing live and watching my audience sing and dance along to my music. It was an indescribable feeling, almost like coming home. I felt I was exactly where I was supposed to be, as if I had finally found my place in the world.

FALLING IN LOVE

EVEN THOUGH MY professional life was flowing wonder-fully, the truth is that I quickly dove back into working like crazy, without stopping or ever having time for anything else. So my mother came to support me while I went through it all. My mother loves Mexico, and the time we spent there together was very special—I was no longer the boy who had returned to Puerto Rico after being an international celebrity, and I was in a more mature place in my life to have a solid relationship with her.

I know many people with incredible mothers say the same thing—but my mother is an extraordinary woman to whom I owe a lot. Not only for the obvious things like raising me, taking care of me, keeping me company, but also because she has always been a great source of support and inspiration in my life. For example, in large part it's due to my mother that I have a great passion for music, in particular salsa, merengue, the boleros, los trios. . . . She is a devoted music enthusiast and she always had hundreds and hundreds of albums at home. And while my brothers and I spent our time listening to classic rock, she would interrupt us to make us listen to some music from our island. In fact, she once took us to a Fania All-Stars concert, something for which I am beyond grateful! Even though she didn't necessarily convert me to Latin music back then, later on these influences would have a profound effect on my career. When we lived in Mexico, she would always bring me CDs of artists, such as Fania, Celia Cruz, El Gran Combo, and Gilberto Santarosa, and slowly but surely it was through those recordings and all the way from Mexico that I began to appreciate the richness of my island's culture. All thanks to my mother.

There were still a few years before the renowned Latin Boom would emerge in music, the phenomenon that propelled my career, but the seeds of what was coming had already been planted. However, just as my professional life was gradually taking direction, my love life was in total flux. Ever since I had left Menudo, I had shared experiences with both men and women, none of which lasted long enough to even be considered a relationship. Shortly after I'd arrived in Mexico—while I was working on the play—I met a wonderful woman who was the host of a very successful television show, and from the moment I saw her I was attracted to her. Apart from being one of the most beautiful women I have ever met—tall, blond, and as elegant as a first lady, with the style, poise, and class of someone like Coco Chanel and the beauty and sensuality of a Brigitte Bardot—she is a brilliant woman, sweet and caring. We quickly started dating, and she soon became my partner, my friend, my everything. What we had was something magical, and I would have sculpted a throne for her, because to me she was the perfect woman. I loved feeling her body against mine and her hair as it caressed my chest while she was totally disconnected, in her own world, our world. She loved me, and I loved her, and we had many moments of complete and total union. She was an incredible woman. Actually, the perfect woman.

But like most boys of that age, I was not ready to be with the perfect woman. I was too immature. That, along with the thousands of issues that swirled around in my mind, made me unable to commit to her or even to myself. She could have been the love of my life, but in that moment I felt I had more experimenting and living to do. Or at least that's how I justified it to myself when we were no longer together.

After we broke up I spent a couple of years acting like

the typical alpha male, a total ladies' man. I was young and famous, I was an artist, and I made it my business to go out with every woman who crossed my path. It didn't matter if she was single, married, widowed, or divorced. What I wanted was to have a good time and live to the fullest. I wanted to get to know myself and give myself the chance to try new things. I don't know if at the time I wanted to prove something to the world, or to myself, or if I was simply allowing the situation to flow with all the fury and euphoria of adolescence. During those years I also had some experiences with men—part of my experimentation—but they were never relationships that lasted or marked my life in any way. They were fun, exciting, and I enjoyed myself immensely, but in the aftermath they always left me feeling guilty, so I decided I didn't want to think about them. I did not allow myself to analyze or assess whatever was going on inside. I was living through so much and having so much fun that I focused more on *feeling* and less on *thinking*.

I was in the middle of this whirlwind of relationships when I fell into the grips of passion with a marvelous woman who was intense, sensuous, and also forbidden.

She was the complete antithesis of the first woman I mentioned, but just as strong, with a lot of personality and confidence, with a very unique perspective on life. Everything about her seemed larger than life—she was a megawoman. The thing is, I didn't just like her a lot; this woman drove me *crazy*. In a matter of days she turned me into mush: She lit up my soul and turned me inside out. She was like a poison that awoke the animal in me. The attraction, desire, and physical passion I felt for her tore me up in every way. Physical chemistry overload. The smell of her body was completely addictive and her skin, sweat, tongue, her excitement, the way she moved, the way we both moved together . . . The whole thing drove me insane. She hated her breasts, but they made me crazy. I loved looking at her body; it was like a painting that I could describe to the last detail. Her legs and the little toes on her feet lit me up. I wanted to devour them—and I always did. I was obsessed with and fascinated by everything about her. She was simply incredible. The time we spent together was like a roller coaster; she awoke a rebellious streak in me, a craziness, and a spontaneity that opened me and liberated me, and to this day I feel that it was one of the most electrifying relationships I have ever been in.

I was so obsessed with her that I allowed myself to entertain all kinds of dreams and illusions about a future together. But sooner or later, I would come back to reality and ask myself, "Come on, don't you see that you are just a toy for her to play with? Enjoy it while it lasts!"

The fact that she was married—although at the time she was separated—was of course a source of constant pain for me, but I think it was also part of what attracted me so much. Forbidden attraction makes things more exciting. And she was both dangerous and a forbidden woman, which made the whole thing even more irresistible. But despite how much I loved her—and maybe because of it— she broke my heart. One day when she picked up the phone and heard my voice, she said, "Oh, Gabriel, I have a headache right now; I'll call you when I wake up."

This response was like a bucket of ice thrown in my face. Pretending I was Gabriel, her assistant, meant that she was sleeping where she was supposed to be sleeping—with her husband. In that instant I told myself, "This has gone to shit." I hung up the phone without saying a word and just sat there. Freezing. I was so hurt. I was living through a moment that I had known would come, or to put it in the words of the great Gabriel García Márquez, it had been "the chronicle of a death foretold."

I will not deny that it took a while to get her out of my mind. Despite the damage she did, all I could do was think about her. Sometimes I even waited for her at the entrance of the theater where she worked, just to see her for an instant. I did it in a way so that she couldn't see me, of course. I mean, if we must lose our dignity, no need to lose it completely, right?

But no matter how much pain one can feel and no matter how much hardship one may have to endure, life always goes on. There is a Persian saying, "This too shall pass," and it could not be more true.

CITY OF ANGELS

SHORTLY THEREAFTER I got a call from my agent telling me that NBC wanted me to move to Los Angeles to act on a TV show. Even though Mexico had brought me many extraordinary things, and to this day I have many friends there whom I adore, I think I was ready for a change. The prospect of moving to Los Angeles came at the perfect time. I had been in Mexico for almost five years. A lifetime for someone like me who had been on the road almost constantly.

The first show I appeared on for American television was called *Getting By.* Sadly, the show was quickly canceled, but I did not have much time to worry because I would soon discover that I had once again chosen the right path. When that show was canceled, I was free in Los Angeles. What could be better for a young artist wanting to get ahead in show business? I didn't have to wait very long, because one day my agent called and said that the executive producer of *General Hospital* wanted to meet me.

The irony is that it was not through my role on *Getting By* that she discovered me, but because she had attended one of my concerts and loved it. Once again, music was opening the door to a world I was not even looking for.

In the United States, unlike in Latin America, soap operas last for years until one day they stop getting good ratings and are canceled. While in Latin America the soaps go on for a few months—a year at the most—in the States they can go on almost forever, and often tell the story of several generations within the same family. *General Hospital* is one such program that has lasted for years, and it is one of the most popular soap operas in the United States, undoubtedly one of the most famous. I was shocked when they called me, not only because it was a great opportunity, but also because it seemed like they had already decided to hire me. They had me read a few pages of a script in front of various ABC executives, but it was just a formality, so that later no one could say I hadn't auditioned. A few hours later, I officially joined the cast.

I was given the role of Miguel Morez, a singer who ran a bar during the week and on the weekends spent his time singing. I played the part for two and a half years, and during that time I learned a lot about what it takes to be an actor. But the part on *General Hospital* did not come without its fair share of challenges. I joined the show because I honestly wanted to break into the acting world in Hollywood. At that time, I believed I wanted to be an actor, and although my role on *General Hospital* could have been a great gateway, I never felt entirely comfortable during the time I was on the show.

When I look back, maybe it was just that I was on another soap opera, but most of the time I felt the work I was doing there just wasn't for me. I didn't feel that I jelled well with the rest of the cast, and there were many times when I felt misunderstood, insecure, as if I would somehow never be able to fit into that world.

The fact that I was treated as a foreigner also did not help. I had already traveled around the world three times by the time I'd arrived in Los Angeles, and everywhere I went people would tell me they loved my accent. But when I got to L.A., I started to feel that my accent was horrible. People told me I should take a class to reduce it, or would comment on how strangely I pronounced this or that word. Whatever they would tell me I am certain their intentions were not bad, but even so I felt insulted. Excluded. Different. Maybe back then it wasn't as common as it is today to have Hispanic actors on TV, and people were not used to seeing people who weren't like them. I don't know, but it was a very unpleasant feeling for me.

Besides feeling uncomfortable with my work situation, there were all kinds of other things that were messing with my head. It was around that time that the universe put another great love in my path—one of those loves in which you immerse your entire body and soul, and this time it was a man, for whom I almost gave it all up.

We met at a radio station, and from the moment we met it was like a meeting of souls—at least that's the way I saw it. I was traveling outside L.A. at the time and came to the station to do an interview. As soon as I opened the door of the studio my eyes met one of the most beautiful gazes I have ever seen. He was a very handsome guy, of course, but I had already seen plenty of handsome guys in my life. This man had something special, very special; it was magnetic. It was as if we had known each other for a long time. He interviewed me for his program and I kept asking myself, "Am I getting a vibe from him, or am I imagining it? If what I am feeling is true, I am diving in without fear." At one point when I was answering one of his questions (he later confessed that he thought his questions were really stupid because he was so nervous he didn't know what else to ask me), I stared at him steadily, and when I saw that he did not turn his gaze away . . . *Boom!* He confirmed what I was thinking. We exchanged phone numbers. He began visiting me in my hotel. We both loved music, as well as art and literature, and we spent our time talking about so many different things. At one moment I would tell him something about music, while he said something about literature, and later perhaps the roles would reverse. We had a really intense physical connection, and intellectually we were just on the same frequency.

When I visited him, we were literally inseparable. At night, he would go to work at the radio station, and I would stay in bed listening to his voice, while he would send me subtle messages over the airwaves. It was especially meaningful to me because I had always been the one who did the pursuing. I don't know if it is because of what I represent that the people I am with can sometimes be a bit intimidated by me, but when it comes to both women and men, I'm always the one who makes the first move. Honestly, no one had ever sent me coded messages over the radio before! It was very original and very romantic. During the days I would do whatever I could to be with him and court him, but at night he would counteract on the radio. Without anyone else noticing, he would play certain songs and say certain things that only I could understand. He would scream his love out to me over the airwaves, but the really incredible, powerful, magnificent, and devastating thing about it was that only I knew it.

After a few weeks I returned home, but we continued our relationship at long distance. It was not easy because on most weekends one of us would have to get on a plane and travel for several hours to see the other. But I loved him a lot. Once I even suggested we both run away and leave everything behind to go live together somewhere . . . Asia, Europe, anywhere. We were young and I truly felt that the best thing we could do was to leave our worlds behind and move in together. I didn't care about my career or what would happen if I told the whole world I was gay. Nothing else mattered.

But he didn't feel the same way.

"Ricky, you have a very clear mission in life," he told me. "You move masses. You can truly impact people. You are at a point in your career where you are so much more developed than I am. I still have a lot of work ahead of me, and if something bad were to happen between us, you would inevitably blame it on this, on me, on the fact that I held you back. . . . And I can't let that happen."

At the time, his words deeply moved me, but I still tried to convince him, by all means possible, that we had to at least try. But he refused. In the end, I think he was right. I've come to believe that he simply wasn't ready for the relationship I wanted us to have.

It might just be that I loved him more than he loved me, or maybe he still had to find himself in several other aspects of his life. Who knows. The fact is, we shook one another; while I was with him I stopped fearing my sexuality, and I was ready to confront it and announce it to anyone and everyone who was willing to listen. It was because of that relationship that I came out to my mother. When it was over, she noticed I was very sad and she asked: "Kiki, are you in love?"

"Yes, Mami," I answered, "I am completely in love."

"Aaaaah," she said. "And is it a man that you are in love with?"

"Yes, Mami. It's a man."

When the relationship ended, I told myself that maybe

this was not my path. My soul was in pain; I felt abandoned, alone, broken. So much pain didn't seem natural, so my instinct was to convince myself that being with men was a mistake. I locked my feelings even deeper inside, and started to date women again, with the hope that with one of them I would finally find true love. Even though my instinct tells me to wonder what would have happened had I decided to accept my sexuality at that point in my life, in reality I see that it did not happen this way because it was not my moment, and there were still many things for me to live before I would get to that point.

IDENTITY CRISIS

THE RELATIONSHIP WITH that particular man taught me a lot about emotions, but in the years to come I learned even more. I learned that it is very easy to lose yourself in the pain. Pain comes, it seduces you, it plays with you, and you identify with it to the point that you start to believe this is how life is. When you feel that heaviness in your heart, most of the time the parameters of pain and relief become blurry, and it is very easy to stay stuck in what you already know, pain. We lose our memory and forget the peaceful moments when everything was light and gravity was an ally. It's okay to feel hurt—it's human. It's important to feel, but you cannot cling to sadness, distress, or bitterness for too long, because they will inevitably destroy you.

Something a friend once said to me helped me a lot: "When you feel stuck and everything feels heavy, struggle!" It's so true. You have to struggle. You have to feel.

You have to move forward. When I am not feeling my best, emotionally speaking, the last thing I want is for people to know how I am feeling. My grandfather always told me, "Go through life with your hands in your pockets, making fists so everyone will think that they're full of money." What he meant was that you should never let people see you down. I think that lesson stayed with me, because to this day I would rather not be seen at all than to let anyone see me when I'm feeling down. I am a very private person, and I have always lived through my joys, pains, and struggles only with a few people who form my innermost circle. Of course I live, feel, and suffer, but it doesn't make sense to carry my pain around everywhere I go.

But that said, today I feel I know how to be aware of my pain, and to work through it, spiritually, with strength and confidence. Throughout my life, I have little by little acquired the spiritual knowledge I need to do away with whatever hurts me, and move forward only with the things that nourish me.

Of course, I know there is always room for improvement, but at the very least I know I have stopped fearing pain. If I encounter it in my life—and I know there will always be pain and that there is no way to eradicate it—I know what I have to do to face it and overcome it with strength and confidence.

However, when I broke up with this man, I was feeling very lost, and all of the energy I had invested in loving him was now invested in thinking. I overanalyzed everything. I tried to make sense of what had happened to me. What I felt for him was very strong, very intense, but now that he was no longer by my side, I was left to face the terrifying abyss of my sexuality. I didn't know what to do with all of those feelings; I was afraid of their intensity and I was scared that I had felt them toward a man. Just as I had built up the courage to come out of the closet in order to be with this man, his rejection solidified all my doubts and fears. I already felt it was hard to be a Latino in Hollywood; what could have been more difficult than being Latino and gay?

It was a very profound moment in my life, when I was trying to decide who I was. And the more I thought, the more I rejected myself, because I could not give in to my true nature; because my true nature was not compatible with my goals and vision. Even my career was going through an identity crisis: I didn't know if I wanted to be a singer or an actor, and even though I was fortunate enough to be a working actor in Hollywood, the truth is that there was something inside me that was resisting the entire experience.

Inevitably the moment came when I felt I just couldn't take it anymore. I needed a change. I needed to escape. I felt that Los Angeles had overwhelmed me. So I called Wendy Riche, the executive director of *General Hospital* at the time, and one of the most wonderful people I met during my time in Hollywood, and I told her, "You might say I'm crazy, and honestly, I am feeling a bit crazy. But I need a vacation and I need your permission to cut my hair."

Back then I had long hair, and in my contract there was a clause that said I could not change my image in any major way without first obtaining permission from the show's producers.

"*What?*" she yelled. "Oh, my God! Continuity! If you cut your hair now, you'll appear with short hair in one scene and long hair in another. . . . For the love of God, Ricky, don't do it!"

The scene was even funnier because I was calling her from the hair salon.

"I'm going to do it!" I said to her.

"No!" she yelled back.

The hairdressers were cracking up. It was honestly very funny, if also a bit sad, because my hair wasn't really the problem; it was my identity I was struggling with. I was like a little boy throwing a temper tantrum; I had gotten it into my head that I wanted to cut my hair, as if that was going to solve whatever angst I had and no one was going to tell me otherwise (or so I thought!). Fortunately, after debating it for a while, I saw things differently and decided to listen to Wendy.

Even though I had to leave my hair long—if only for a few more days—I did get two weeks of vacation out of it. And considering how hopeless I was feeling at that time, those two weeks of freedom meant a *lot*. I used them to go to the mountains, where I rented a cabin to disconnect from the world. It was February and very cold; on some days I would ski, and other days I would stay home and read, write, think. There was a telephone, but I'd use it only sporadically to call my family or friends to let them know I was okay.

One day, after several days of being alone, I had the urge to climb a tree. I think I climbed that tree because I remembered that when I was a little boy, I used to climb into a tree that was in front of my grandmother's old house. I would take my *Star Wars* figures up there and spend hours creating great battle scenes in space. I don't know if it just made me remember my childhood, or if it was because I had spent so many days in silence, but all of a sudden I began to cry uncontrollably. I cried and cried for a long time, and slowly released all of the angst that had been building up inside me. Finally, when I calmed down, I returned to the cabin, where, a little while later, the phone rang: It was my father, calling to tell me that my grandfather had just passed away.

While I was up in that tree, crying and remembering the tree of my youth, the tree that was such an innate part of my grandfather's world, he had passed away! I realized that all things in life are connected and I could no longer go about life without looking within. That moment affected me profoundly, and it awakened something in me on a purely spiritual level. Even though I did not know how I was going to do it, in that moment I felt the need to connect deeply with a force or energy greater than me. It was a moment of great turmoil, but when I look back on it today, I see it as a very important moment, because it marked the beginning of a crucial spiritual journey I am still on to this day.

MAKING MUSIC

BEFORE I ARRIVED in Los Angeles, I had already released my second album, called *Me amarás*. Since the first album sold very well, some 500,000 copies, the record company decided that for *Me amarás* it would be important for me to work with one of the most respected producers in the industry, Juan Carlos Calderón. Juan Carlos is an exceptional person, whom I respect and admire profoundly. From the day we started working together, I felt very grateful for the opportunity to collaborate with him. For me it was a learning experience to work with someone of his stature, but if I am honest, I always felt that that record was more his than mine. I lent him my voice. I liked the album and it received positive reviews from the critics, but it was not the sound of Ricky Martin, and although the album was still really good, musically speaking, the audience was mostly responding to that.

When I listen to the record today, even though I think my voice back then sounded very different from how it sounds now, I still feel immensely proud of the production. It would have been perfectly normal to feel frustrated by the experience or disappointed that the album didn't sound like my own, but I think even in that moment I had the perspective to understand that *Me amarás* was merely one more step in my career, and not what would define it. Sometimes the experience is worth more than the end result itself, and this was one of those cases. The experience of working with Juan Carlos was in itself amazing—I learned a lot from a musical and technical point of view—but it also helped me to realize that I would never again make an album that did not feel like my own. When you are surrounded by so many talented people, it is normal to start doubting your own artistic choices, but to be a truly original artist, it is crucial to stay true to yourself. And that was the lesson I learned. My third album would have to be completely my own.

I began working with K. C. Porter, an amazing producer, and Robi Draco Rosa, an ex-colleague of mine from Menudo. Draco was always a very talented musician, singer, and artist. He was someone whom I'd always admired and it was nice to see how destiny had played out—to reunite us after so many years. Draco has since produced various records for me. Just as he once said in an interview: "Ricky Martin and I are like Julio Iglesias and Sid Vicious." What he does with me has absolutely nothing to do with what he does with his own music and his performances onstage, and this is a musical versatility not many artists possess. He knows exactly what I need and when I need it. From that first collaboration with Draco and K. C. Porter, *A medio vivir* was born. This was the album, released in 1995, that featured the famous "María," a song I am extremely proud of—and which was, at the end of the day, the song that made me a star and changed my life forever.

In life, there is always the temptation of wanting everything at once, like right *now*. When we chase a dream we see it all so clearly, and it's normal to want it to become a reality right away, or at least as soon as possible. But as we all well know, things in life are never simple. The path toward one's goals is often full of obstacles, and by overcoming each obstacle in your own way, there is a lesson to learn. If I had not learned everything I learned during *Me amarás*, perhaps I wouldn't have been ready to collaborate with Robi and K.C. and accomplish what we did together on *A medio vivir*. It was an album that would change my life in many ways, although I didn't know it at the time. So by the beginning of 1996, my career as a solo artist was starting to really take off, but I was still missing one critical step before fully coming face-to-face with my destiny. This time the call came from New York, specifically from Broadway, where I was invited to perform in the popular musical *Les Misérables*.

I am an artist because I love music and I adore the stage. In this sense, musicals seamlessly fuse my two passions, acting and scene work with music, which is why some of the most magical moments in my life occurred when I was asked to perform on Broadway. It was an incredible challenge, and every night I was surrounded by supremely talented individuals in an atmosphere of absolute creativity. I made it my point to take it all in and enjoy every single moment.

Like so many other things in my life, *Les Misérables* came to my life totally unexpectedly. It was thanks to an interview I did for the *Miami Herald*, in which I was asked, "What have you not done yet that you would really like to do?"

Without hesitation, I had answered: "I'd like to perform in a Broadway play."

I said it because it was of course true, but I would have never imagined what came next. A few days after that interview was published, I got a call from Richard Jay-Alexander, the associate director and executive producer of *Les Misérables*. He told me he had read the article, and with very little preamble he offered me the role of Marius Pontmercy.

Once again, I was not required to audition. They didn't even test me—nothing. They simply handed me the role. And of course I accepted right then and there.

Many people might think it is a question of luck. But more than luck, I believe that after almost fifteen years of working like a madman, the time had come for me to reap the benefits of all my efforts.

Thus began eleven extraordinary weeks before a packed theater, fully booked night after night. I was later told that tour operators from Latin America even organized trips to New York so that their clients could see me in the show. What an honor! I think that was the role of my life, and if they offered it to me again, I would take it in a heartbeat. It is common to hear some of the great Hollywood actors say in interviews that their favorite roles have been on Broadway, and honestly, I can completely relate. It is a very intimate and challenging experience, so it does not surprise me that it is something that many dream of doing again, again, and again.

Some eight years after I performed in *Les Misérables*, I ran into Richard Jay-Alexander at a restaurant in New York.

"Marius, my Marius! You'll always be my Marius," he exclaimed. "Ricky, I gotta tell you the truth: Victor Hugo wrote that character for you."

I could not believe what he was saying to me. Richard is a knowledgeable guy, and he has some of the highest standards in the industry. Never mind knowing what it takes to put on a show like this one! I was very flattered by what he thought of me.

SEARCHING FOR GOD

DURING THE SUMMER I spent on Broadway, I met a Hungarian girl who was a hairstylist on the show. We spent hours talking and I really liked her. I felt like my heart skipped a beat each time I saw her. I tried to ask her out in every possible way imaginable, but she would always give me the same response: "I can't go out with you until we go to church together." And since I liked her a lot, I said, "No problem, let's go." So I went.

Since it was summer, the church held its services in the park. I had to get up at seven in the morning—seven in the morning on a Sunday!—because the services started at nine. I went to pick her up and we walked across the park until we reached the spot where the services were held. But as soon as we got there, she disappeared. Lots of nice young men walked up to me and welcomed me to the service, but she was nowhere to be seen. Suddenly I realized that all the men were standing on one side and all the women were on the other side. I thought it was very strange, but I was there because I wanted to get to know this girl better, so I went along with it.

Even though I came to the church because I was courting a girl, I also feel that I arrived there because it was what I needed at that moment of my life. I spent a little more than two months going to church, reading the Bible, and studying religious subjects. Even though I grew up

Catholic, I'd never really *studied* the Bible, and it was here that I truly discovered how wise Jesus Christ was, and the great beauty of his teachings. My life until this point had been total craziness, and the simplicity of those moments shared with all those other young people made me feel so good. It was a very peaceful atmosphere, very wholesome, and it helped me to get closer to the little boy inside me.

In the teachings of Jesus Christ I found a very important concept, self-forgiveness. Back then, I was constantly struggling with all the "bad" things I thought I had done. I'm talking mainly about physical desire, whether for members of the same sex or the opposite sex. Back then I thought those types of thoughts were impure and not okay, which is why I really needed to forge a sense of forgiveness toward myself. And this brought me a monumental calm. This church also taught us to see all human beings as "our brothers" in order to put an end to any kind of physical attraction. That worked for a little while, because I honestly did not want to feel what I was feeling, and I didn't want to have the thoughts I was having, which, according to "the faith" and certain social codes, constituted the devil's temptation.

The church began to govern my life, and I even got to a point where I considered getting baptized, but ultimately didn't do it. It was hard for me to change my way of thinking, given the values that were etched in my mind—at the end of the day, once a Catholic, always a Catholic—but I honestly tried to.

As I progressed in my studies, I began to ask myself more and more questions. I read the entire Bible, until in one of the groups I was attending, someone said, "If you don't repent for your sins and accept Jesus Christ as your salvation, you will not enter the kingdom of heaven."

The affirmation hit me hard. I said, "Hold on a second. What do you mean by that? You mean to say that everyone I have loved intensely who has passed away is not in heaven if he or she did not accept Jesus Christ as their salvation?"

"Well, yes," they answered, "we have to pray a lot for those souls."

I was stunned. My grandparents were saints. They were people who dedicated themselves to helping their fellow human beings. They adored their children and were devoted to their families; they never lied, and never showed malice toward anyone. Their lives were filled with love and generosity! And these people were telling me that because my grandparents did not go to church they are not in heaven? If this was the case it was clear to me that I no longer wanted to go to heaven. I wanted to be wherever my grandparents were.

I started to ask myself other questions: What happens to the other people who don't share this faith? Are they not in heaven, either? I thought (and still think) these kinds of affirmations are seated in a great deal of arrogance. Where do the Jewish, Muslims, Catholics, Buddhists, Taoists, Native Americans, atheists, agnostics go? Are they trapped in nothingness? I think my questions were very valid. They might seem a bit abstract to some, but they were definitely valid to me.

I was faced with what for me was an irreconcilable conflict. I continued studying and I began to find other things that made me feel uncomfortable in the teachings of this church; for example, the church's stance on homosexuality. Even though I did not know yet that I was a homosexual—or to be more precise, I was trying with all my might to convince myself that I was not—I knew that some of the people I loved were homosexuals, and they were certainly not bad people, unworthy of Christ's love. All of these realizations made me very nervous; I became preoccupied and anxious. Finally I realized that this is not what Christianity was about. I had spent months reading about the history of Jesus, and noticed that in addition to His teachings, there were a series of laws created by humans that didn't always make sense to me. If Jesus Christ was a compassionate being, it made no sense to say that the people who do not believe or act the same way He did are wrong, or destined to enter the gates of hell. Also, deep down inside I felt I was being attacked on a personal level when they said, "If you're a homosexual, you are the son of the devil"; that bit just didn't work for me.

What a horrible irony. They attack me, but they love me; they accept me, but they exclude me. They speak of homosexuality as something that can be "cured" through prayer and atonement, as if it were something bad, when in fact homosexuality is a blessing the same way heterosexuality and life in general are blessings.

It got to a point where there were just too many contradictions. So I stopped going to the church and understood that another chapter of my life was closing. I am grateful for the things I learned during those months, but I realized it was not giving me all the answers I needed. I had many spiritual moments, but also many clashes. It was another step on the path, another lesson. My spiritual journey was only getting started and I had many steps left to take before I would find the peace and acceptance I needed.

With time I have learned that life has a funny way of shaking me around when I need it most. In that moment, I don't always understand it, and often I even resist it, when in reality I have learned that what I need to do is open myself up to the challenges that lie ahead—because it is these very challenges that allow me to grow, learn, and change. Instead of resisting change, I have chosen to search for it and embrace it because all change, as scary as it may seem, comes with an infinite realm of new possibilities.

Destiny is a curious thing. It doesn't always take us where we want to go, and many times it ends up taking us to an unexpected place where we feel confused, lost, with no idea where to go next. These are complicated and painful moments that make us suffer and question who we are, along with what we want the most in our lives. But if we really make the effort to see these challenges as opportunities to find ourselves, we will understand that it was exactly what we needed to discover and strengthen our role on this planet. That is how I see it, and that is how I face every opportunity and every challenge that life brings me.

I believe that everything that happens in life happens for a reason. I also believe that the God that lives inside me—to call it something—is in charge of giving me everything I am going to ever need. All of my joys and pains have made me who I am. They are the yin and yang of my existence, this inseparable duality of life that blends together and makes us the people we are destined to become. I have known love and loss, joy and sadness, friendship and betrayal. I have known a sense of success I never imagined possible; I have had to withstand the attacks and accusations of my detractors; and yes, I have also had failures. Today I know that every step has taught me something and helped me grow and become a better and stronger person—a more complete human being.

It has been incredible to sit back and think about everything that happened after Menudo. I was running in circles when I did not know what I wanted to do with my life. But gradually my path began to reveal itself and I discovered how life itself was leading me toward my goals, finally, to my destiny. As it was happening, I did not always understand why I had to experience what I had to, but with time I could see that everything had its own reason. I could finally see that a single experience—good or bad—does not define everything, and the most important thing is to always stay alert to the various opportunities that arise. Every course has its fair share of bumps, and as painful and hard as they may have been, these bumps were crucial for my growth and maturity as a person and an artist. I still had a long way to go, but after *Les Misérables* I finally felt that I held the tools to move forward. I felt strong, powerful, and invincible. The small bumps I had faced paled in comparison to the sense of triumph for having been able to develop myself creatively as an artist, in genres as different as television, film, theater, and music. All of these experiences gradually shaped me into a much more complete person than I was when I left Menudo, and they taught me that the most important thing is to remain loyal to one's self and live with the conviction that each and every one of us is destined for something extraordinary. This was only the beginning.

THREE

MY TIME TO SHINE

THERE ARE SOME PEOPLE WHO BELIEVE THAT WE SHOULD not have everything at once, but I disagree. Instead, I feel we should not have everything until we are actually ready. And to become ready, one must work. A lot. I'm not just referring to practical work, the type that helps us to reach the professional success we seek. I am also talking about spiritual work: We must learn from the karmic lessons that life places on our path.

In my life there was a moment when the stars aligned perfectly and everything was in the exact spot where it needed to be so I could reach the goal I'd always dreamed of, and beyond. And if I learned anything in the process, it is that when your moment finally arrives, you cannot allow yourself to get held up by looking back. You have to work tirelessly, give it your all, and dedicate your heart and soul to actualize the blessing that has been given to you. Because it is just that—a blessing. We have to grow in response to the circumstances, and make the most of our chance to shine.

My fame in the world of entertainment did not come unexpectedly. Even though it may seem to audiences in some countries that I showed up out of nowhere and started selling albums like crazy, the reality is very different. My rise to the top of the charts as a top-selling artist came after many, many years of hard work and dedication by both myself and my entire team. From a very spiritual and personal point of view, I had taken the time to discover what I wanted to do with my life and which direction I wanted to take. I felt ready and strong, prepared to face all the challenges life might dole out. But despite being ready for everything that was to come, I would never have been able to imagine the scope of it and how that would affect each and every area of my life.

TAKING THE WORLD BY STORM

THE RIDE BEGAN in the fall of 1995, with the release of my third album, *A medio vivir.* The first single released was called *"Te extraño, te olvido, te amo"* ("I Miss You, I Forget You, I Love You"), a ballad that was in line with the kind of music I was making at that time. But the album also had a secret gem: a song called "María." On this song we fused Latin rhythms with pop, and it had a tempo and vibe that was distinct from everything else on the record, but it was also completely different from anything else I had ever done. I knew there was a certain amount of risk in releasing such different material, but the results spoke for themselves: "María" was the song that propelled me to the next level.

The shocking part is that the first time I played the song for a record label executive, he said, "Are you crazy? You have ruined your career! I can't believe you are showing me this. You're finished—this is going to be your last album."

I remember that whole thing felt completely surreal. The guy completely exploded, without any real reason and without giving me the benefit of the doubt. I couldn't believe what I was hearing, and needless to say I was devastated. Even though I really liked the song we produced—I loved it, actually—hearing those words from the mouth of a high-ranking label executive made me doubt myself and the work I had done. This guy is not even a musician, so I'm sure he didn't have the slightest clue about what it takes to lock yourself up in a studio and make music, everything you go through, emotionally speaking. But to me making music is a very personal process, so I felt he was attacking me at one of my most vulnerable moments, and I took everything he said very personally. I even got to the point where I imagined my career was essentially over, and that I would never again be able to make a record or perform live on a stage; nothing like this had ever happened to me before.

But despite the fear this horrific man planted in me, I remained silent. I didn't say one word, not to him and not to anyone. I went through a few days of anxiety, but my consolation came a few days later when the boss of that hateful individual selected the song to be released as a single. The rest, of course, became history. "María" became a bestselling single in France, Spain, Germany, Belgium, Holland, Switzerland, Finland, Italy, Turkey, and all of South America, where from the moment of its release it shot straight to the top of the charts. By the start of 1996 it was among the top ten bestselling singles, and I put it to the test when I performed it at the Viña del Mar International Song Festival, where the famous *monstruo de la quinta Vergara** did not devour me. To the contrary: The song was a smash hit, and it hit hard.

It was very exciting. When we saw how well the song and the album were doing, we set off on a tour all over Latin America. At the end of the tour, I returned to New York, where I went straight into my role as Marius Pontmercy in *Les Misérables*, and lived those extraordinary weeks in the theater. There, something very interesting happened. As I was onstage each night on Broadway, people all over the world were singing and dancing to the sound of "María." The song then crossed the Atlantic and reached Europe via Spain. During the summer and fall of 1996, the song continued to gain momentum, and it was thanks to it that I held a concert on Avenida 9 de Julio in Buenos Aires, Argentina—which is like performing in the middle of Times Square in New York or the Champs-Élysées in Paris. We were expecting a lot of people, but could have never predicted that over 250,000 people would show up! It was incredible, and we had a blast as I became one with the audience. The footage we shot that day was later immortalized in one of the videos for the song "María." The Argentine audience was amazing, and I'll remember that day for

---

* The audience at the Festival de Viña del Mar in Chile is the only one in the world to receive a special name—"*el monstruo.*" This creates an expectation in people who attend the show. They wait for the slightest opportunity to show their displeasure, shouting catcalls at performers who are not to their liking, sometimes even booing them off the stage. When that happens, they say jokingly that "the monster ate" the artist.

the rest of my life. The warmth of the reception I received from that incredible audience not only made me feel accomplished as far as the work I had done, but it was also a clear indication of everything that lay ahead.

The now infamous Latin Boom wouldn't hit yet for another couple of years, but that same month, the Argentine newspaper *El Clarin* was way ahead of the trend when they published a piece about the Latin fever that, according to them, was starting to sweep through the United States. I was mentioned as one of the artists introducing Latin rhythms to audiences that couldn't speak a word of Spanish. Later, when the Latin Boom hit with full fury, thundering through every inch of the planet, the article turned out to be prophetic.

Back then, and thanks in large part to the phenomenal concert we did in Buenos Aires, I felt I had the full support of the Latin American audience. Many of my fans knew me from my days in Menudo and we had all grown up together. Others were new admirers who only knew me as a solo artist. The support of the Latin American audiences has always been a source of great inspiration and pride for me, but at that moment, with everything that was going on around me, I felt that something huge was just about to happen. I wanted to broaden my horizons and reach new audiences throughout the world, including the United States and Europe. And the more I seemed to want it, the more opportunities began to pop up.

My career was on the rise and I was not going to let anything get in my way—not even a car accident in the mountains of Italy.

In 1997 I had the honor of being invited to the prestigious music festival of San Remo. We landed in Milan, where we were slated to board a helicopter to San Remo, but when we reached the mountains the sky closed in and the pilot said: "We're not going to make it. I am going to land the helicopter so that you can continue by car."

We didn't have much time, and the last thing we wanted was to be disrespectful by arriving late. So the moment we landed, we continued by car at top speed in order to make it on time. The truth is we were going very fast, some 120 miles per hour, the wheels screeching with every turn. Suddenly we arrived at a turn where the car just couldn't take any more, and it turned upside down! But just as I said, I wasn't going to let anything get in my way. As soon as we made sure none of us had more than a couple of scratches and bruises, we grabbed all the equipment and looked for a taxi. We finally made it to the red carpet, slightly shaken but on time. "Everything okay?" we were asked. "Yes, yes, yes!" we answered. "Perfect." My agent later told the press that the car had slipped and we lost control in the rain—though the truth was a little worse than that. But we weren't going to let a little car accident jeopardize our presence at such an important European music festival!

As "María" continued to top the charts around the world, many people started asking who this famous "María" might be. They wanted to know if she was someone I knew or wanted to know. Everyone had their own theory, and people's theories were hilarious! For example, Charly Garcia (a music legend in Latin America; I call him the Great Master of *Rock en Español*) said in an interview, "I believe Ricky

Martin is eulogizing drugs." You see, the song's lyrics say that "This is how María is, white like the day . . . and if you drink from her, she will surely kill you." And for Charly Garcia, this phrase apparently referred to cocaine. Wow. The fact that Charly Garcia would even talk about one of my songs in one of his interviews was a huge honor. That the Great Master of *Rock en Español* would even notice my music was a sign that I was doing something right.

It goes without saying that Charly's theory was not correct. I sang and danced and performed it at so many of my shows, but until Charly drew the connection to drugs, the idea had never even occurred to me! His interpretation completely changed the way I saw my song. And that is exactly what happens when you put a song out into the world: It becomes everyone's property and everyone has the right to interpret it and live it as they see fit. Later I'd laugh, because the truth is that once you dive into the subject of cocaine, there is plenty of material to go around.

Whether people danced because they thought the song was in praise of drugs or because they thought they knew the María who the song was about, the one sure thing is that everyone who heard it danced to it. And that was a lot of people! That summer I did a concert tour in Spain, a run of forty-five shows in thirty-six cities. Then in December I gave four concerts in France and Switzerland, starting in Paris. "María" was already one of the top ten songs there and in Italy. It also received a gold record in Switzerland, Sweden, England, Belgium, and Greece. The song unfurled all over the continent, and I followed it. In total, the album *A medio vivir* sold over 7 million copies around the world, an astounding figure when compared to my previous sales. Later, concerts and chart-topping hits followed in many more countries, and in each case it was "María" that would continue to open doors for me.

As "María" took the world by storm, in 1997 I returned to the studio to record my next album. Like everything else in life, music has its own trajectory and everything has its moment. I wanted to release another album before the public's enthusiasm for *A medio vivir* started to dissipate, but I didn't want to disappear completely in the process. So I continued doing the concerts and the ongoing promotion in new markets for *A medio vivir* while I recorded *Vuelve (Come Back)*. It was brutal and incredibly intense. When you're recording an album, you need a certain amount of space to concentrate, think, and connect with your creative being. But when you are on tour, you need to give it everything you've got. The permanent contradiction between these two states was, for me, totally draining.

And I couldn't rest long because soon another door opened. When we were almost finished with the recording of *Vuelve*, I was contacted by FIFA: They wanted to know if I was interested in creating a song for the 1998 World Cup, which was slated to take place in France. I have to admit that the challenge made me a bit nervous, but the massive growth potential for my career was such that I decided to accept. Once again, life was offering me an opportunity and I swiftly ran to meet it.

Right away, I joined forces with K. C. Porter and Robi Rosa, who had worked with me on *A medio vivir* and were now working with me on *Vuelve*. But for the World Cup song, we were also joined by Desmond Child. From that moment on, we began to look at the album as part of a global strategy to promote Latin music worldwide, so we chose and arranged the songs with the sole mission of getting the entire globe to dance and sing in Spanish. It was a unique opportunity to introduce the charms of Latin music to the rest of the world.

And that's how we embarked on that adventure. The single that resulted from that collaborative effort was *"La Copa de la Vida"* ("The Cup of Life"), and it served as the official anthem of the 1998 World Cup. It was a huge success that hit number one on the music charts in more than sixty countries. Another indication of what the future would hold.

Vuelve was released in February of 1998, and in April I started a concert tour through Asia, which began in Tokyo. More than one year later, when I was starting to wrap up the tour, a journalist from *Rolling Stone* magazine asked me: "Why did you choose this path? Why Asia and Europe before the United States?"

The answer was easy: Because this was the path that life had offered. All I had to do was follow it.

The night of July 12, 1998, was one of the most important nights of my career, and the entire time I was fully aware of how much was at stake. It was the World Cup final. Not only were there hundreds of millions of people watching me perform "The Cup of Life" on television in all the corners of the world, but some of the most recognized and respected names in the entertainment industry were right there in the famous Stade de France. Among them were Dustin Hoffman, Arnold

Schwarzenegger, Michael Douglas, Luciano Pavarotti, José Carreras, and Plácido Domingo. My performance was scheduled for immediately prior to the game, and would only last for four minutes. That meant I only had four minutes to turn one quarter of the world population into fans, or possibly lose them forever.

Before the show I was very nervous. Despite the fact that I had performed tons of live shows in front of hundreds of thousands of people on stages and in theaters throughout the world, this was the first time I had done anything quite so epic. And no matter how much experience you may have, a stage like the Stade de France on the night of the World Cup final is beyond intimidating. It was almost unimaginable!

Besides, what no one knew—except for the FIFA officials and a group of my closest friends—was that my performance during the ceremony almost didn't happen. At some point, FIFA had told me that there was a chance I might be able to perform at the final, but before they had a chance to confirm it, I went ahead and announced it to the press. *Bad call.* FIFA, of course, was supposed to make the announcement, and my faux pas made them angry. Very angry. Instead of either confirming or canceling my appearance, they decided to punish me by leaving the whole thing unresolved—until five days before the game, and the whole time they didn't say a word about my performance to me or to anyone else. I, of course, was dying. I really wanted to perform, and I didn't want a stupid announcement to the press to ruin that chance! They finally gave me the green light, but with one condition: For the show I would have no stage, no dancers, no lights, and no special effects. I would have none of the things that are standard for a concert of this caliber. I was supposed to do a global performance without a global production, or any production at all.

But I was so happy to hear that they had confirmed me that I didn't really care about anything else. What mattered most to me was to perform, and I knew I would find a way to turn it into something spectacular.

And that's exactly what we did. At the last minute it occurred to me to assemble some twenty musicians and dress them all in white shirts and black pants, so that the audience could see them from far away. We all came out onto the soccer field, all of them playing their instruments, and I grabbed the microphone and yelled out to the crowd: "Come on, let's make some noise!"

When we got to the center of the field all nervousness disappeared and the magic of the event took over me. It was four minutes of pure euphoria. The stadium was filled with people from all over the world on their feet dancing to the music. Hearing the crowds clapping and screaming, I felt a massive surge of joy and strength. That performance, for me, was a singular experience . . . a gift sent to me by life. Another moment I will never forget. Absolutely everything was in place, and the crowd's adrenaline made me understand the reason for all my efforts and sacrifices. We had worked like savages to get to this moment, and the victory was now at our fingertips. I broke my knuckles busting down walls so I could get into Menudo, become a solo artist, and gain the support of Latin American, Asian, and European audiences. And the applause and screams on that night at the World Cup were the beautiful acknowledgment of all that arduous work.

But there was no time to rest on my laurels. All of the acknowledgment I received in France was extraordinary, but we had to keep moving forward. We just couldn't stop and accept the glory as a matter of fact. When life gives you an opportunity, you have to give it your all and then some. You must fight and struggle to forge your own path. Which is exactly what I continued to do.

CROSSING OVER

AFTER CONQUERING ASIA, Europe, and Latin America, I set my sights on the United States and on my so-called crossover—my transition to the English-language marketplace. And to keep the momentum that we had going, we decided that while I did the promotion for *Vuelve* with a forty-four-concert tour, I would also return to the studio to work on my first English-language album. This time I didn't care what I had to do; my goal was to achieve everything I set out for myself. That meant I had to give it my all, and that's how it would have to be. The months when I promoted *Vuelve* while simultaneously recording in the studio were incredibly intense. Granted, I had already done something like this when I recorded *Ricky Martin* while simultaneously shooting *Alcanzar una estrella*, and when I recorded *Vuelve* as I promoted *A medio vivir* . . . but this time the record I was making demanded a lot more from me. With the success of *"La Copa de la Vida"* there were many more requests for interviews and autographs, and I always tried to have a friendly, positive, and energetic attitude about it. I'd agree right away. If they needed me for a magazine photo shoot, I'd eagerly say yes. If they wanted me to sign a giant pile of CDs, "Of course!" I would eagerly respond. If they would request interviews, it was always, without a doubt, a yes, yes, yes, but it was exhausting.

I said yes to everything because I wanted the entire world—and more than anything, the United States—to notice me. That crossover to the American market meant so much to me that I was willing to do anything at all to make it happen. But despite all the enthusiasm with which I pursued my new goal, I could already see the dangers that lurked behind it. With the success of "María" and *La Copa de la Vida,"* I had already seen a glimmer of what fame as a solo artist was really like, and I didn't like it one bit. I remember I even mentioned this in an interview I did around that time for *El Nuevo Herald*: "Every day that passes," I said, "I am more and more fearful of fame." It was ironic, I explained; the more I knew it, the more it scared me. And the more it scared me, the more appealing it was to me.

In the depths of my soul I knew I needed to take some distance to rest and think about everything that was happening to me, but somehow it never seemed to be the right time. In fact, at one point I wanted to take a sabbatical. I had it all organized; the plan was to disconnect for a little while and go traveling, but just at that exact moment, while we were in Singapore on one of the tour stops, my agent called to let me know that *Vuelve* had been nominated for a Grammy Award. And that wasn't all: The organizers wanted me to perform live on the night of the awards ceremony. So despite the rest and relaxation I may have needed, how could I possibly say no? It was out of the question. An invitation to perform on the Grammy Awards show is an extraordinary honor, which many artists never receive in their entire career, and I simply could not say, "So sorry, gentlemen. Thanks for thinking of me, but I'm about to go on a little vacation." It might have been the right thing for me to do from a personal and emotional point of view, but it certainly would have been career suicide. There were so many people who had placed their bets on me—including myself—so many people who had worked non-stop for many years to turn my dreams into reality, that I couldn't say no.

If the World Cup had been my platform to take on the rest of the world, the Grammy Awards would be my entry into the English-language market of the United States. At the time, I didn't care so much that the show was going to be broadcast to millions of viewers in 187 countries; what mattered to me was that I would be able to share my music with the people of the United States who had never even heard my name. Just like the World Cup, this was my moment to shine, and I would only have a few minutes to make an impact: My performance had to be nothing short of electrifying.

I have always thought that it's totally normal to be a bit nervous before a show. In fact, I even think it's healthy, because if I weren't nervous it would mean that what I am about to do has ceased to be challenging. And how interesting can life really be when we are not challenging ourselves and jumping out of our comfort zones? But in the case of the Grammy Awards, as the night of February 24, 1999, got closer, I realized I was feeling worried, stressed, and had a sense of panic. I doubted whether I would be able to impress the audience, if they would like my music . . . until I finally just had to put an end to all of these mixed feelings, and say to myself, "Hold on! You've been at this for fifteen years. So just do your thing—and do it well!" I allowed myself to remember that, which is how I found the strength I needed to perform with my usual confidence. The show turned out well. Great, actually. I've been told that what took place that night had never occurred before in the history of the Grammy Awards. I'd decided to sing a slightly modified version of *"La Copa de la Vida,"* to which I had added a few new lines in English. And this time— unlike at the World Cup—we had a gorgeous stage and set with all the critical bells and whistles: musicians, dancers, lights, and special effects. It was a spectacular show in every possible way, and I gave it all my energy, charisma, and all of the emotion I had to give . . . and then some! We had the musicians walk toward the stage through the aisles of the auditorium, which immediately connected the audience with the music, and they started to applaud and dance at their seats. When we were playing the last note, that crowd—which was made up of professional musicians, composers, singers, artists, and executives—gave me a standing ovation and cheered for me as I had never, ever seen before. I was completely blown away by their intensity—it was like receiving a blessing from an audience that I respect immensely. And it was another moment I will remember for the rest of my life.

When the applause finally simmered down, the cameras cut to Rosie O'Donnell—the host of the show—who seemed stunned. She was quiet for a moment, and then, under her breath, she said: "Who was *that* cutie patootie?"

Just a few moments later I returned to the stage to accept my first ever Grammy Award for Best Latin Pop Music Album, for *Vuelve*. The first thing I did was laugh, probably because I too was still a bit stunned, and then I said, "I got a Grammy!" Once again, the audience reacted extremely positively, and I was stuck somewhere between elation and shock. They were probably wondering, "Who is this guy?" It was the first time most of the audience members had ever seen me, and now I was onstage receiving the record industry's most prestigious award!

Even though awards are not everything, being able to stand before my peers and the world with the Grammy in my hands and to have the opportunity to thank everyone involved with the album for their hard work and dedication was very exciting. So many people put their talent, time, and effort into the making of an album that publicly thanking them when receiving an award is always a beautiful way of showing them the gratitude they rightfully deserve.

And if that wasn't enough for the night, after the show, while I answered questions for the press backstage, Madonna came and stood behind me. She covered my eyes with her hands and gave me a kiss. "I'm just here to congratulate you," she said. And then she disappeared as quickly as she appeared. Wow! Madonna! That, I could never have imagined.

But once again, there was no time to take it all in, or rest, or even celebrate. Instead of basking in the glory of my "Grammy moment," that night I jumped on a plane to Italy because I had a previous commitment—a perfect example of how chaotic my life was at that time.

THE AVALANCHE

I HAD WORKED for fifteen years to earn those four minutes on the Grammy stage, which had allowed me to accomplish my goal—to shake up the American music world and open the minds of English speakers to the rhythms of Latin music. Around that time, the *New York Times* stated that I had "lit the fire of pop music" and that my performance at the Grammys had established me as the "symbol of the new status Latin culture holds in mainstream America." You see, during this time, the Latino community of the United States was growing at an impressive rate, and my musical success to a certain degree was reflecting—and feeding off of—that very change. Latin culture was beginning to seduce the United States and modify the musical preferences of its inhabitants.

Just a couple of months after the Grammy Awards ceremony, I released my first album in English, entitled *Ricky Martin*, just like my first album as a solo artist. It debuted at number one, and sold over 660,000 copies in the United States alone during its first week out, breaking a record.

Not only was it the bestselling album that week, but it had one of the best ever sales in just one week of the whole year. I never expected the album to be so huge; even though I had been getting ready for this moment my entire life, when it finally arrived, it took me by surprise. From a professional point of view, I was completely ready to go that far and even farther, but on a personal level it shook me at my very core. It was all so much and so fast that I didn't know where to look. Life came at me like an avalanche.

First it was the Grammy Awards, with the spectacular show and my first Grammy. Then, the release of my first album in English, and then almost immediately the single "Livin' La Vida Loca" debuted as number one on the charts in twenty countries. That year, the song hit number one on *Billboard* magazine's list of national sales, number one on the national broadcasting charts, number one on the Latin American broadcasting charts, number one on the Latin sales charts, and so on. Later, the promotional tour kicked off with serious impact: It was a whirlwind of autographing CDs, interviews with the press, photo shoots . . . an explosion! And finally, it was time to begin the concert tour. The response was unbelievable. The tickets for twenty-five shows in the United States went on sale on the same day and they all sold out within just eight minutes, literally as fast as the ticketing systems allowed. As a result, we had to add additional shows in many of the cities, and the tour was not only extended in the United States, but turned out to be massive globally as well. About 4 million people came to see me live on that tour, and in total the album sold close to 17 million copies worldwide.

And the avalanche continued. It didn't matter if I was tired or if I was hungry or if I simply wanted to take a nap. Whenever I said, "I need a rest," my manager would come back with, "Just one more little thing. One more, that's it." It's not that he was a bad person, but the problem was that there was always some other little thing to do! And since every little thing we did would yield such tremendous results, I always wanted to do more. For example, one day they'd come to me and say, "Ricky, Pavarotti called. He wants to do a duet with you." Who could turn down the honor of a duet with Pavarotti? So the answer was yes. It was such an honor! I always accepted. Then shortly thereafter I'd get another call saying, "Ricky, Giorgio Armani called—he wants to have dinner with you." Mr. Armani— of course I simply couldn't say no. I would always say, "All right, I'll do it this time, but please don't bring me any more offers." My manager would promise never to do it again, but later he would come back and say, "Ricky, I am so sorry. I know I told you I wouldn't bring you anything else, but the thing is that Sting called and he wants you to perform at this benefit concert he's holding. . . ." What could I possibly do? Who in their right mind could refuse these types of invitations? In the midst of all that madness, "Livin' La Vida Loca" turned out to be everything that Sony Music had hoped for and more. At that time, the company was having financial troubles and they needed more than a good hit—they needed a home run. With the promotional push that they gave "Livin' La Vida Loca," they expected something explosive, and the result was more on the lines of nuclear. Seeing their salvation within arm's reach, they wanted to go as far as possible, so they created an aggressive and extensive global promotion campaign. The only problem was that the one person who would ultimately have to bring it to fruition would be me. And although it was exhausting, I can honestly say I never complained. I gave myself entirely to the task and lived the whole thing like a dream.

Oftentimes people ask me what I think made the success of "Livin' La Vida Loca." Even though part of it was that the world was ready for something new, more than anything, I think that all of the pieces were perfectly in place. I had a wonderful agent, an excellent record label, and a fantastic production team, and all of us were tapped into the same frequency and the same mantra of winning as we moved forward. And in addition to that, I had a great album in my hands; when I listen to it today, I realize what an amazing production it really is, and in the end, that's really what is most important: *the music*. Music can transcend borders and break down barriers between people and cultures. In this case, it spoke for itself.

I would go so far as to say that during the process of recording the song we actually made magic. For "Livin' La Vida Loca" I had the good fortune of working once again with Draco Rosa and Desmond Child. Although I had made several records, I quickly realized that working with Desmond Child is working at an entirely new level. Desmond is a musical giant: He has sold 300 million records; he has worked with Aerosmith, Bon Jovi, Cher, all the greats. When it comes to recording, Desmond has a certain dynamic and unique sense of focus: He somehow turns the process of recording into something structured and systematic, which gave us great calm, because this way we didn't get tired and could allow the creative process to flow. We would start the day by doing vocal warm-ups. Then we would eat something. Then we would do some recording. Then we'd go out for a stroll. And then we'd come back for a cup of coffee. Every day I knew what to expect, and that helped me a lot because I could focus my thoughts on my creativity, as opposed to wasting them on the uncertainty of what's going to happen tomorrow, or the day after. It was also the first time Draco ever worked with Desmond, and there was something about that collaboration among the three of us—the cosmos, the moment, the risks that were taken—that made for extraordinary results. And even today "Livin' La Vida Loca" is one of the songs I am most proud of.

When I think back on the months that followed the album's release, what I remember is work, work, and more work. The wave that had started to grow with "María" and *"La Copa de la Vida"* transformed into something gigantic. I had to gather all my strength to make videos, go on a promotional tour, put on a show, and dedicate myself day and night to promote it. We planned three months of shows and events in Japan, Thailand, Australia, France, England, Spain, Puerto Rico, the United States, Canada, and, of course, Mexico. Since my fans were all over the planet, we ultimately made it a world tour that lasted over a year, with two hundred and fifty shows in eighty cities and thirty-five countries.

That year, "Livin' La Vida Loca" was nominated for four Grammy Awards, putting me at the forefront of the phenomenon that was baptized "the Latino Boom." It was no longer just about the advancement of my own career; it was now about the new and unexpected presence of Latin music on the global stage. My life would never be the same again.

THE LATIN POSTER BOY

AFTER THE GRAMMYS it almost seemed like overnight everyone in the United States had awoken and heard the name Ricky Martin for the first time, which was a bit odd, especially when you take into account that *Vuelve* had earned a platinum record in the United States, with more than 1 million copies sold, outselling some of the most famous names in American rock. But this was proof that in those days, for the most part English-speaking Americans had no idea what was going on in the Spanish-speaking music world.

Only two weeks after the album's release, I appeared on the cover of *Time* magazine, under the headline "Latin Goes POP," and according to that article, I was at the forefront of a new generation of Latin artists who expressed their culture in English. The article observed—and with reason—that a great part of our success had to do with it being the right time. In other words, the Latino community was growing at a monumental rate in the United States, and this growth was translating into Spanish-language radio stations, television channels, and newspapers. Latin culture was penetrating American culture on every level, and the very fabric of American society was beginning to change. It was in those details that I began to recognize the auspice of my life: Had I been born at any other time, even only ten years before or ten years after, it is possible that I would not have had the same success and my life would have played out very differently. But that's how my life has always been—things always come at the precise moment that they should, including, apparently, the moment of my birth.

One month later I appeared on the cover of *People*, one of the most popular and powerful entertainment magazines in the United States, with an article that talked about my "instant fame." Of course, in the eyes of the American media I was someone totally unknown who had just landed on the U.S. musical stage. What they didn't know was that I had a fifteen-year career under my belt, and that the worldwide recognition I had accomplished—this fame they spoke of, this scary new summit where I now found myself—was a result of a calculated strategy. The promotion of the album was planned by the record label to give the biggest possible push for what they saw as a product: "Ricky Martin." As Desmond Child once put it: "Ricky is a prince who has been prepared to become a king."

It has never bothered me that my career had been planned with a very clear strategy in mind. What did bother me at that time was discovering that the media had designated me as the representative for all Latinos. I feel very proud of being Latin, but that certainly does not mean that all Latinos must be like me, nor will they necessarily identify with my music or sense of aesthetics. So from the first moment that my fame started to increase, I felt somehow responsible to break stereotypes and explain to the world that although we come from the same continent, not all Latinos are the same.

There is so much ignorance toward Latin American culture. I have met individuals who, upon hearing that I am Puerto Rican, say: "Yes, of course, Costa Rica!" Or they might look at me and think I'm Italian. When my music began to hit in Europe, I gave a lot of interviews in which I spoke about my culture and how it is manifested in my music. I also took advantage of this opportunity to speak about the differences. For example, in certain parts of the world, some people were shocked to see me show up without a mariachi hat. They believed that everything Latin, from Mexico to Patagonia, is the same and that we all eat tacos and sing *"rancheras"* (typical Mexican songs). So, I would make an effort to explain that Latin America is multifaceted, with many different cultures; even on the same island, you will find several different cultures, accents, musical styles, and rhythms. I cannot say that my music is 100 percent Latin, because it would be an insult to all the rest of the Latino musicians around the world. In Latin America there is salsa, merengue, tango, rock, vallenato, cumbia, son, and many more genres that have developed throughout the continent, and my music is a blend, a fusion, of the various styles since I am not an artist who strictly adheres to one style or another. Of course, my music has Latin influences, but it also has Anglo-Saxon and "europop" influences. So to say that I am a Latin *singer* is okay. But it's wrong to give my music the all-encompassing label of Latin music, or to imagine that all Latinos are, or sound, like me.

When my music started to become popular in the United States, everything happened at once. Thanks to all my touring and promotions, I was already known around the world as an international artist from Puerto Rico. Before arriving in the United States, I had done a sixty-concert tour, including shows in New Delhi, Bangkok, Seoul, Taipei, Singapore, Malaysia, and Australia. I did shows all over Europe. And everywhere I went I was known as "the international artist." But when I arrived in the United States, I was "the Latino phenomenon." I would always go out of my way to say that although I am Latino—something I'm very proud of—I don't represent all Hispanics, as I am my own version. What some people don't know is that although I am Latino, I have French, indigenous, and African blood. . . . In truth, I am a mestizo, as most of us are on the American continent. The fact that I am considered Hispanic is a happy coincidence. One part of my family came from Europe and landed in the American northeast, and today they are considered Caucasian. But another side of my family landed on my island, Puerto Rico, and for that reason I was considered "the Latin phenomenon."

In fact, many Americans, perhaps the majority, know very little about Latin culture and their knowledge is often based on a number of prejudices and preconceptions that are completely wrong. So even though my first cover on *Time* was great, after a while I stopped liking the whole "Latin Goes POP" thing. But to this day, this has made me work hard to project a positive image of Latin culture and show the world that we are more than just a simple label.

FALLING APART

MY FAME CONTINUED to grow. Tens of thousands of people showed up when I held an open-air concert in Rockefeller Center in New York as part of NBC's morning talk show, *Today*. So many people came that they stopped traffic in the center of Manhattan. And there were countless magazine covers and endless attention. I was featured on the cover of *Rolling Stone* swimming in a pool surrounded by naked women; the dream of all rock and pop musicians—it was the ultimate stamp of my success.

That same year, "Livin' La Vida Loca" received six nominations for MTV Video Music Awards, and on top of that, the song was nominated for three international awards at the same event. In total, I won five of the nine awards for which I was nominated, and once again the public gave me a standing ovation when I sang the song live at the awards show.

From a professional point of view, it was one of the best years of my life. And to conclude it, on my birthday, *Entertainment Weekly* named me artist of the year. I had reached such extraordinary heights that I could even begin to doubt how I could go any higher. Just as I said in an interview during that time, what could I possibly do after this? Climb Mount Everest?

Well, I did not have much time to sit and ponder the question, because the record label quickly informed me that they wanted another album as soon as possible. Now, when I think about it, I realize I should have said no. *Definitely no!* It was too soon and I was not ready to fully immerse myself in the intense creative work needed to record a new album. But I was so busy working and making an effort to do everything I had to do to keep the wheels in motion, maybe I didn't have the time or the distance to really evaluate what was being asked of me. The label said they would need a new album, so I simply went along.

It was one of the worst decisions of my life.

It was absolute craziness and a very serious mistake. But it was my decision and I decided to go through with it. Some say I should blame my advisers or the record label for pressuring me, but the truth is it was all my fault. This wasn't Menudo anymore and I was no longer a kid who was being told what to do. I was a grown man and I had been working in the music industry for many years, yet I agreed to do something I did not want to do. The only way to learn in life is by making our own mistakes, and that was one of the mistakes I learned most from.

So we started to prepare the next album in English, called *Sound Loaded*. Every week I had four or five consecutive days of concerts on the "Livin' La Vida Loca" tour, and after the last show, I got on a plane to return to Miami, where I locked myself up in the studio to record. We worked until the break of day; then I would sleep a bit. I'd wake up and return to the airport to get to the next stop on the tour, right on time to do the sound check for the show. Many of my friends in the industry said this was crazy, that this is not how it was done.

"When you are making a record," they'd say, "you're supposed to do only that."

"Ha!" I would answer. "Who says?" I had done it several times and I was doing it again.

As soon as the concert tour was over, we began the promotional tour for *Sound Loaded*. A typical day began by waking up when my plane from Australia, for example, landed in L.A., where I had to record greetings for radio stations in Orlando, Detroit, Miami, and other major cities. Then I had to give a series of interviews for the press before doing a photo shoot for the magazines. It was a furious schedule that never stopped. Every day began at dawn and ended late at night. I almost never had a free afternoon or morning to simply take it easy. I could barely breathe.

In some ways I felt like the king of the world, and that feeling, although it came with a certain level of exhaustion, was also intoxicating. I liked to feel the power I held in my hands, and above all else, I loved being able to harvest the fruits of our labor of the last fifteen years. But there were also moments when I was afraid of what my new lifestyle could bring. Sometimes I felt I wanted to escape back to my little island and live in a little house on the beach with a hammock facing the ocean, and other times the only thing I wanted was to go out and party, rent out a whole nightclub, invite my friends to dance and flirt with the paparazzi. Every day I would shift between those two extremes: between wanting to escape everything that was going on around me and wanting to give in to it entirely. On the one hand, I felt wonderful and greatly fulfilled; but on the other hand, I was in pain, and the feeling of constant change was driving me crazy.

I believe that very few people around me noticed it, though, because I would do everything I could to hide what was really going on inside me. When people asked me, "Ricky, how are you?" I didn't even take the time to think about it. I would automatically respond: "I am great, thank you very much." But the reality was very different. I had a terrible stomachache, my head was spinning, and I felt a tightness in my heart. I didn't know what I was feeling because I did not take the time to explore it, but what I did know was that I was carrying around a lot, a lot of pain. But I kept saying that everything was okay.

Around that time, I recorded a song with Madonna called "Be Careful (*Cuidado Con Mi Corazón*)," and upon seeing the intensity with which the press followed me, and how willing I was to always promote, she said to me, "Ricky, stop doing interviews. Everyone knows who you are." And that truth struck me like a lightning bolt. It took me some time to process this—and more than that, to apply it to my life—but one day I finally understood exactly what she meant. I had spent so much time focused on doing publicity, being available, and always giving, giving, and giving to reach my goal that I didn't realize that, to a certain degree, I had already reached it, and surpassed it without even noticing. That is when I understood that the rules of the game had changed and that I had to find a way to reclaim control of my time and my life. But that would not happen for a long time, because, like everything else in life, it wasn't my moment yet. Before I found my peace I would have to get to that particular moment when I really just couldn't take it anymore.

Back then, my cardinal rule was to always give as much as possible and then some, because with every little bit I gave, I got so much back, and that would make me want to give even more. Sometimes I say that it wasn't that I was working too hard. I was just giving too much. It's just that the validation from fans is intense. I believed I was ready for that kind of success—after all, I had been in the spotlight since I was twelve years old—but I soon realized I wasn't. I wanted to scream: "Wait! I can't deal with so much. Let me just stop for a moment!"

For a long time, I believed that the success we reached with "María" and *Vuelve* would be the grand culmination of my career. But after the success of "Livin' La Vida Loca," that all seemed like child's play. I always say that things come to my life at the exact moment when they need to, not before and not after, and I receive them with a loving heart. But this time, it was completely overwhelming. I did everything I could do to keep myself moving at a thousand miles per hour, to take advantage of the fantastic opportunity that had been given to me, but it was inevitable that I would get to the point where I would just not be able to take it anymore. And just as it is important to know how to accept things that destiny sends us, it is also crucial to know when to stop and take a step back from that which could harm us. The success I had achieved was monumental and nourished me in a very particular way, but it was also leaving some invisible wounds in its wake that would require some time to heal. All the mania lasted more or less two years, by the end of which I was completely empty and numb. In fact, I didn't *want* to feel anything anymore. I did everything I had to do without thinking, practically on autopilot. The only thing that truly gave me pleasure was being onstage. It was the only place in the world where I felt utterly free. That's where I did exactly what I liked to do, how I liked to do it, when I wanted to do it, and the energy of the audience always fed my soul. That is when I again became Kiki, the little boy in his grandparents' house having a good time, making jokes, dancing and singing. Onstage, I felt strong and free to be who I am, how I am, without any fears or pretenses. But later, when the show would end, I'd rush back home to hide and disconnect. Everything always hurt, and although no one could really see it, internally I was suffering. Most people can't imagine that it is possible to be surrounded by people at almost all times and yet still feel completely alone. Or that being on the road isn't always as glamorous as it looks. After a while, you just want to sleep in your own bed.

I didn't want to go on, but to any proposal that came my way I would always say, "Yes, yes, let's go! I am ready." In some ways, this behavior was a result of my "military training," but I was also clearly trying to escape from the pain I carried deep inside. As long as I was always working, I had no sense of what I was really feeling. Deep down I was afraid of what I might find. So I'd concentrate on what "I had to do" and just kept moving forward.

Today it is very easy to see where this path was leading me. I realize that with *Sound Loaded* many mistakes were made and many decisions were hastily made. It was way too soon to come out with another album. In fact, it was so soon that when the first single was released, many people thought it was a song from the previous album, *Ricky Martin*. After the megasuccess of *Ricky Martin*, it was important to let some time pass before releasing a second record. I should have stopped, even for just a little bit. However, the record label needed its next hit, and when they pushed me to do it, I didn't say no. I didn't really want to stop, because stopping would have forced me to think about all kinds of things I did not want to analyze.

FOUR

TAKING CONTROL
OF MY LIFE

BEING AN ARTIST MEANS YOU ARE CONSTANTLY LOOKING for the approval of others. Be it in music, writing, painting, or dance, art, by definition, seeks to interact and connect with its audience. For me, this is a fundamental aspect of what I do. The moments I am happiest are when I find myself on a stage, surrounded by my musicians, and facing a massive audience that is worked up and genuinely excited about my music. I love feeling that the people enjoy my music, that it means something in their lives, and that we are in some way connecting. When someone likes what I do, that feeds my soul.

There are artists who say they create music or make their art for themselves, and that the public's approval is irrelevant. Even though it is a point of view I fully respect, I don't share in this belief. I am a performer because I love my music and I love to dance, but if no one else liked it, I wouldn't feel so good. Call it ego, fear of failure, the need to be accepted, or whatever you like, but I honestly feel that music has to create a real *connection* with the world around it.

That's why, when "María" took off, then *"La Copa de la Vida"* and later "Livin' La Vida Loca," I was overjoyed.

All of this work, the travel, the hours spent in the studio, giving interviews, photo sessions . . . I was now reaping the rewards of all the work and I felt deeply that I was living through a uniquely extraordinary moment, a veritable blessing. However, that moment—the moment I had longed for with every last bit of my will—brought with it a whole series of challenges I was perhaps not ready to face. To a large degree I was already used to doing what other people expected of me: At the onset of my career, when I always followed the band managers' instructions, and later, when I did the same for the theater and television directors with whom I worked, with the record producers, the label executives . . . I spent so much time following the advice of others—most of it well-intentioned, thankfully—that without realizing it, I had begun to lose my own identity. I so badly wanted things to go well and to reach the success I had always yearned for that I seldom stopped to consider if I could realistically do—never mind *want* to do—everything that was expected of me. The years of my rise to fame were an amazing era for me—there's no doubt about that—but they were also the years when I felt I was beginning to lose sight of where it was all going.

RELENTLESS SCRUTINY

GUIDANCE FROM THOSE who have walked the path before you is very valuable, and another piece of useful advice Madonna gave me was, "Ricky, if music, art, or your career start to take over your life, disconnect. You have to be the one who controls your career; don't let it control you." Of course, Madonna is a very wise woman, and I totally got what she meant, but it was hard for me to put it into practice.

The year prior to the Grammy Awards, I didn't feel that music or my career controlled me. The entire world was listening to my songs and I felt I was at my peak, in full control of everything that was in the works. Even so, there were things that gave me a bit of anxiety. I was completely focused on doing everything I could to maintain the extraordinary momentum that had gotten me to this point, but there were still moments when I felt that the workdays were too long, simply because I was incapable of saying no. My manager would show up with an itinerary and I would say yes to everything, without ever stopping to consider the consequences. I was, of course, enjoying my success, but I can't stop thinking that maybe I was also trying to escape from the heavy emotional burden I carried. Just like when I was in Menudo, when I focused on work all the time because, to a certain degree, I wanted to escape what was happening between my parents, during the craziness of "Livin' La Vida Loca" I think I was also trying to avoid the ever-lurking contradictory emotions regarding my sexuality. To a certain extent, being busy all the time meant that I didn't have to think about uncomfortable things.

It was around that time that I again started to date the wonderful woman whom I had met in Mexico. Being with her always gave me so much peace. There was a lot of love and attraction between us and I felt safe with her. I felt cared for. Focused. During all the time I spent with her, I never looked at anyone else. I never even wanted anyone else, and our relationship really made me feel anchored. It provided me with a stability that I had been missing from my life for a long time, and it allowed me to keep a distance from the attraction I felt for men, which always made me feel so guilty. I felt great when I was with her; I loved her and felt loved by her, so there was no reason for me to think about anything or anyone else.

But the illusion that I had my career and personal life under control didn't last long. My relationship with this incredible woman lasted a little while longer, and after a lot of back and forth, we broke up for good. It's hard to explain what makes a relationship end, and although I clearly see today that my own inner conflicts had a lot to do with it, there are other factors that made us drift apart, and we finally decided—always with a lot of love and affection—to separate.

And that's when I began to lose control.

While my team and I worked nonstop to keep the whole operation moving smoothly, with promotional tours, concerts, and videos, all of a sudden, my personal life became a constant topic for the media. Naturally, the public wanted to know who this Ricky Martin was, this guy everyone was talking about, and so they started to ask. In every single interview I gave around that time, people wanted to know where I was from, what my childhood had been like, what my parents were like, if I had someone special in my life. . . .

There is a fundamental difference between movie stars and singers that most people don't realize. When an actor promotes a film, interview questions generally revolve around the actor's role in that project, the film's subject matter, and the on-set experience; there is a countless number of subjects that can be explored without having to make the artist's personal life the central topic of the conversation. However, when it comes to a singer, there is a much smaller range of topics to be discussed, and the conversation tends to focus on the artist's personal life, which is ultimately the inspiration for his or her music. The questions tend to be more personal in nature, especially when, as in my case, the music depicts themes of love and romantic disappointment.

Since I never said no, there were interviews with me in every single magazine, on every television show, and in every newspaper. My videos were on MTV every ten minutes. In the interviews I said very little about my private life, and since what I did say gave them very little to talk about—I was a healthy guy, a hard worker, with no vices—I suppose there were some members of the press who were intent on discovering my "dark side."

And that's how the rumors started. I have no idea exactly how they began, or who may have said what, but the fact was that stories started to crop up in the tabloids saying that I had been with this or that guy—ironically, none of them was true, even though I was, in fact, having relationships with men. I understand that rumors sell magazines, and often this is what people want to read, but the truth is that the invasion into my private life hit me like a ton of bricks. I couldn't understand why I had become the target of so much speculation. All I wanted was to continue with my music and live my life without anyone meddling. I had naively believed that despite being a celebrity, I still had a right to my privacy.

The rest of the world didn't think so.

THE COST OF DENIAL

IN TRUTH, THE problem was not so much that there were rumors going around about my sexuality. The real problem was that I myself did not know how I felt about the subject. Even though I had relationships with men after separating from my first love, I still was not ready to accept myself as gay. My moment had still not arrived, and even though we all know now that the rumors were based on truth, the reality was that in my mind it was still not a fact. It was a topic I constantly struggled with, one that caused me a lot of pain and anxiety. And every time someone wrote in an article that I was a homosexual, or each time this was asked of me in an interview—and not very subtly—it pushed me further away from my truth. The rumors and questions only increased my insecurity and my self-rejection; they reminded me of all the reasons why I was uncomfortable in my own skin. At times I felt I hated myself. Because it was always presented under such a negative lens, as something scandalous and bad, it reinforced my desire to deny what I was feeling. And since at that moment I was so far from being ready to come out, the only result was that the whole thing caused me a serious amount of pain.

Years later, a biographical documentary was made about me for television, and they interviewed a lot of people from the industry, as well as music journalists. In that piece, they said something I think is very astute: When such a huge phenomenon as Ricky Martin hits the music world, it attracts a great deal of envy and a lot of hatred as well. It's sometimes referred to as "player hating." Joe Levy, who was the editor of *Blender* at the time, couldn't have said it better: "When a pop star is too well-dressed, too well-groomed or is too perfect, it is as easy to hate him as it is to like him." It's possible that some people wanted to dig up some gossip about me, or say something that in their eyes might be negative, for the simple reason that they didn't want me to do well. Whatever the reason may be, the fact remains that for me it was a time of great anguish.

I believe one of the factors that contributed to the rumors about my sexuality was that people maybe thought my image as the "Latin lover" was excessive. In other words, perhaps they thought that everything I did—the way I danced, the lyrics to my songs, my sexy onstage moves— was nothing but an attempt to conceal my homosexuality. And this is where I feel the need to clarify: I am the artist I am thanks to the many experiences that have influenced me along the way, and this has absolutely nothing to do with my sexuality. Even though I know very well that all my music and performances have a "sexualized" component, inasmuch as I dance with women, move my hips, and enjoy the rhythm, that doesn't mean it is an expression of my sexuality, regardless of whether I feel attraction for women or for men. When I am onstage, I am always looking for a way to connect with the audience, and if I discover a hip movement or a dance step that people like or get excited about or that gets them going, then I am going to continue doing it. It has to do with the very nature of performance and seducing the audience, which has nothing to do with my personal life.

When I am onstage, I am *working*. I do it with dignity. I do it with respect. I do it because I like what I do and because I want other people to like my music and my performances. In countries outside of Latin America, Latin culture has always had a very sexualized connotation, but that sexiness that others seem to perceive is completely normal for those of us who are from that part of the world. The movements of salsa, merengue, and cumbia exist in all our countries.

Perhaps the moment that encapsulates this whole issue about the rumors and the damage they were causing me was a now infamous interview with Barbara Walters. Renowned for her interviews with some of the most famous and powerful people in the world, she has the unique ability to extract personal details that have never before been revealed. My interview was aired on the night of the Academy Awards, on Sunday, March 26, 2000. At the time I was probably one of the most recognized people in music; and because of all the media promotion I had done for the past four or five years, I was completely overexposed. The album *Ricky Martin* and the song "Livin' La Vida Loca" were still selling like hotcakes, and at the time I was also on a world concert tour. The Barbara Walters special was a much-anticipated segment on TV on a night that has one of the largest numbers of viewers all year.

The interview was conducted in Puerto Rico. After walking a bit on the beach, we sat on a porch for the interview.

She asked me questions about my success, my life as a singer, my family, and like the good investigator she is, when I least expected it, she point-blank asked me the question I feared most: She asked me about my sexuality.

I responded the same way I always answered the question: I told her that this was a private matter, and it was no one else's business. But instead of accepting my answer and moving along with the interview, she stubbornly continued to dig. To a certain extent I can understand that she was just doing her job, but she pushed me pretty hard, maybe thinking that she would be able to get some kind of on-air confession from me for the show. I don't know. But the fact is, I didn't give her what she wanted.

I stayed firm with my answers—as much as possible—but I remember that my vision went blurry and my heart started to race. I felt like a boxer who had just been hit with a decisive punch—staggering and defensive, but already knocked out, waiting to fall. But I did not fall. I don't know how I did it, but I stayed strong. Now, as I write this, I laugh, and I'm not sure if it's a nervous laughter or if it is that with a bit of distance I am amused by the sheer ridiculousness of the whole situation. The fact is, all I can do is laugh.

Years later, Barbara admitted that perhaps she should not have asked me that question and regretted having done so. Even though the past is the past, I greatly appreciated the gesture, because it means a lot to me that she understands that I simply wasn't ready. Even though all the rumors were out there, things were still not clear in my mind, and coming out of the closet simply wasn't an option.

The external pressure only served to increase my angst, and instead of bringing me closer to my moment—the day when I would feel comfortable to reveal my truth to the world—it distanced me even more. Every episode such as this made me bury my feelings deeper, in an attempt to continue to drown out my pain.

Today I think about how easy it would have been to say yes, and feel proud of who I am. Even though I never really lied, I did dodge the question, and I was very clumsy about it. Now I see that it was so simple, that I was drowning myself in a glass of water, but back then I did not see or live through it that way. It doesn't matter how I look at it—the bottom line is that it was not my moment. Why? Because it wasn't. It just wasn't.

The truth is that it was not just for me that I remained silent. Although I accept full responsibility for my decisions, I also felt that I needed to think about how my actions might affect my family, my friends, and all the people around me. I have always taken care of those around me, and I do it because I love to do so. That's how my life has always been, and it genuinely makes me happy. Some people think it's not healthy to be this way, and I agree. It's something I have to work on, but that's just the way it is. It is clear to me that what I do inevitably has repercussions on other people's lives, and in that moment I felt that if I spoke about my sexuality, people would reject me and my career would likely be over. And if my career was over, who was going to support my family? Now, many years later, I realize how absurd it is to have even thought this, but that's how I saw it then. So I continued having relationships with men, but I always kept them hidden. It infuriated me to think that people thought they could walk into my house and see who was in my bed. Regardless of what my sexual orientation may be, I should still have a right to my privacy.

All the pressure from work as well as the media started to become so oppressive that the stage was the only place where I could feel any sense of peace. But after a while, even that started to lose its appeal. For the first time ever, even onstage, I often felt uncomfortable, unsatisfied, and empty. I did not understand why I was doing what I was doing. That's when I said to myself: "Wait! Hold on a moment! This is the only thing you really love to do, and even here you're starting to feel bad? It's time to stop." Performing onstage was the only thing I had left, the only thing I loved about being an artist, and I was even starting to lose that.

I don't know if the general public felt it, but I'm pretty sure they did. In other words, if someone saw one of my concerts in New York or Miami that took place at the beginning of the tour, when I was enjoying myself, and then saw the same show in Australia, when the tour was starting to wrap up, they would have definitely noticed the difference. By the end, I was there and I was doing my job, but the whole time all I was thinking was, "I cannot wait for this to be over so I can just go home already."

All I wanted to do was sleep. I wanted nothing more. So the moment came when I took Madonna's advice and disconnected. We were in Australia and the next stop was Argentina. A stadium full of people awaited us in Buenos

Aires, but I canceled it. I just couldn't take it anymore. This was only the second concert I had ever canceled in my life, and the first was due to illness.

Everyone in the band kept asking, "But what happened? What do you mean we're going home?"

"Yes," I'd tell them, "we're going home. I am totally beat; I simply cannot take it anymore."

"But, Ricky, we only have one more week left of the tour," they would say to me. "Come on, it's just one more week."

Under normal circumstances, I would have made that extra effort and forced myself to use every last bit of energy I had left. But this time it was different, and I knew they would never be able to convince me. I simply did not—could not—go on, and there was not a soul in the world who could convince me of the opposite. All I wanted in that moment was to go home.

I guess it was an anxiety attack. I was tired of everything, and not even the stage was enough to remedy my discomfort. If I didn't want to do the shows anymore, what was the point of it all? I had to stop, because who knows what could have happened to me had I gone on for even one more week at that pace?

I had been working practically nonstop for seventeen years—but the last four had been brutal. First came the tour for *A medio vivir*, then *Vuelve*, and almost right away came the Grammy Awards and all the craziness of "Livin' La Vida Loca." Four years of touring is a lot. It made complete sense that I was feeling this way.

Besides, I didn't like who I was. I didn't like what I was feeling. I started to behave in a way that I had never done before. It's not that I showed anyone disrespect; I didn't scream or yell or do anything like that, but I did begin to lose my discipline. I would arrive late. I played with other people's time. I remember once I was doing a tour through Germany and I had an event at nine in the morning, and I showed up very late in the afternoon. Maybe for other artists that's no big deal, but for me it is. Everyone has their own standards. To me, not showing up at rehearsals or for an event, that's when I can't sink any lower.

So I stopped working. I went back home and isolated myself from the world. I moped around my house and had very little sense of humor and no patience. I would spend entire days at home in my pajamas—which for me is totally out of character, as I have always been quite active, energetic, and wide-awake early in the morning, always ready for the day ahead. But at that moment I wanted nothing to do with schedules, obligations, or appointments. All I wanted was silence.

Now that I look at it, I see that time as the beginning of my metamorphosis. I began to evaluate what I wanted out of my life, what I needed and what I did not. It was like a rebirth. And within that rebirth it was as if I was also going through a process of spiritual detoxification in order to come back to the basics, to return to the calm. I was ceasing to be the person I had been for those last few years, to become a new me. I found it to be a very interesting process, but those who knew me best, my closest friends, simply could not understand what was going on.

One day a close friend came to see me, and shocked to see what was happening, she yelled at me, as if wanting to wake me up from the stupor I was in.

"You're screwed up."

"No!" I yelled back. "This is how I am! If you don't like it, leave!"

"I'm not going anywhere," she replied.

At that, I hurled a glass that crashed against the wall and shattered into tiny little pieces. It sounds silly, a single act of desperation, but the effect it had at that moment in my life was totally unexpected. Instead of scaring my friend into leaving, I was the one who was shocked: The explosion gave me an emotional jolt. In the shards of glass I saw scattered on the floor, I saw what was happening in my life. If I did not do what was necessary to fix this right away, I too would end up shattered in a million little pieces. I didn't recognize myself in such a violent gesture, and I understood that the problem was even more serious than what I was willing to admit. It's one thing to be famous and another thing to be totally controlled by fame. Being famous can be a very positive thing, but being controlled by it is not in the least bit positive. Even though I thought I was escaping it all to be myself, my erratic behavior was proof that fame was still controlling my life.

I don't have any regrets because everything that happened was meant to happen. Did it hurt? Definitely. But I learned a lot. And that's what is important.

ROAD TRIP

TODAY I CAN say I have forgiven myself for allowing myself to sink so low. There are still moments when I think about how I let my life become so out of control, how I allowed myself to be seduced by the fame. Maybe I could have acted and done things differently, but that was the lesson. I needed to face all the challenges that came my way in order to move forward on my spiritual path. I arrived where I did to learn a lesson and not make the same mistakes in the future.

But to come to this understanding I had to hit the bottom of the barrel, according to my standards. This is where I began to look inside to find the path that brought me to my awakening. When that glass shattered against the wall, I saw it all. I immediately began to repair all the damage I had done to myself. It was time to make some major changes. I stopped seeing the people who were a negative influence on me, I got back to the gym, and I meditated a lot. I did a thorough cleanse and embarked further on my spiritual quest. I needed to leave all of the material stuff behind—the cars, the houses, and the private jet I had bought myself—and walk on foot where no one knew who I was, and if they happened to recognize me it wouldn't mean a thing. I had to reconnect with that six-year-old boy inside of me and, as a matter of priority, make him happy again.

I asked myself: Who am I? Why am I here? What is my mission? My happiest memories in life are from my childhood. The time I spent with my father. Going for coffee with my grandparents in the afternoons. Being with my grandmother in her living room as she worked on one of her projects. Listening to music with my mother. Thinking back on those simple times that were so happy, I realized what I needed was to go back to the beginning. I had to go back to being a little boy.

I started to practice martial arts, and within six months I became a bit obsessive: For breakfast, lunch, and dinner I lived and breathed capoeira, a martial art from Brazil. It combines the elements of music, play, battle, and dance. It was like being a kid again. I went to a capoeira academy where people from ages eighteen to forty practiced. But when we were training, we all turned into kids.

I also set aside some time to travel. Along with some friends, I traveled across the United States in an RV. Of course, we could have done the trip in a high-end luxury tour bus, with a chauffeur and every amenity imaginable. But I said no. I didn't want that. First of all, I wanted to drive. And I didn't want to have anything around that reminded me of my work. If I had decided to travel on a big beautiful bus, I'd again be reminded of the crazy tours and having to rush from concert to concert.

In fact, what I wanted most was simplicity. When we stopped, it was not to find a fancy hotel, but instead to look for a campsite, and that's where we would stay until it was time to get back on the road. We would drive in shifts. One day we were driving through a small town in Texas and I was at the wheel. Apparently, I had exceeded the speed limit and a policeman stopped me.

"Was I really going over the speed limit?" I asked him. "In this big thing?"

"Well, yes," the policeman replied. "You were going thirty-five miles an hour in a thirty-mile zone."

I gave him my driver's license, and when he looked at it he couldn't believe his eyes.

"Huh?" he said. "Ricky Martin? Here?"

"Yes," I said, resisting the urge to laugh.

"But what could Ricky Martin possibly be doing in this little town?"

We spoke for a while, I told him about my vacation, and I asked him how to get to a motel. Later that evening I cracked up just thinking of how his family and friends at the police station would probably not believe him when he told them the story.

And that's how the whole trip went. From one town to the next, without any luxuries or fanfare. I went with one group of friends, and along the way we met up with other groups of friends who lived in the various cities we passed through.

I traveled through the Grand Canyon, Las Vegas, Vail, Aspen, and the Mojave Desert. I went where I wanted and did what I wanted, with very little planning. I enjoyed the whole thing very much.

For the first time in a long time I felt completely free, powerful, able to do whatever I wanted, regardless of what anyone said or thought of me. I had spent so much time only thinking about work, about what was expected of me and what I had to do each day that I had forgotten what it was like to wake up in the morning without a fixed plan.

I also went to Asia a few times. I went to India on a trip that would change my life. I came back. I spent some time in New York and later went to Brazil in search of new sounds. I went to Egypt with a few friends, always trying to remain anonymous. I'd wear a hat, and when we arrived at the hotel, one of my friends would check me in and I would go straight to my room. Every day I would go out and people would look at me, saying, "Could it be him? No. It can't be. . . . But it sure does look like him."

One day in Egypt, we hired a guide to take us to the historical and tourist sites and explain to us what we were seeing. As we walked around she would look at me from the corner of her eye, but during the entire tour she didn't dare say a word. At the end of the afternoon she couldn't resist any longer and she asked, "Excuse me, sir. Are you Ricky Martin?"

Yes, I am. But not the one you know.

Now I am Kiki, nice to meet you.

Things were changing. Now I felt the need to dedicate as much time as possible to the little boy within me. I felt that I had to disappear for a little while and go deep inside to connect with my truest emotions, my deepest sense of self. I fell in and out of love, and I allowed myself to fully live through these relationships. With more calm and less fear, with less blame and more acceptance. I learned to love myself again and to be the spontaneous and joyful boy I used to be.

THE JOY OF SILENCE

THE FIRST THING I did when I returned to work was record an album in English, which would be the first to be released since *Sound Loaded*. But it took forever to make. So when I was about halfway through, I stopped recording in English and went back to recording in Spanish. From that, *Almas de Silencio (Souls of Silence)* was born, with the song *"Asignatura Pendiente"* that I quoted earlier. I believe that album, and more specifically that song, are dedicated to the little boy inside me. The experience of making that record without any pressure, to make the album I wanted to make, that was a gift for Kiki. Actually, Arjona's song *"Asignatura Pendiente"* pays tribute to that little boy, and the song comes from everything I lived through during those months.

For *Almas de Silencio* we didn't go on tour, which was something totally new for me. Instead, I went to Europe, Asia, Australia, and Latin America, only promoting here or there—all of it on my terms, without any pressure. I also did some promotion, and somehow or other the album ended up selling close to 1.7 million copies in the United States alone and received platinum records in Spain, Argentina, and the United States. Of course, this does not compare to the success of *Vuelve* or *A medio vivir*, but I felt satisfied because it was a record I made with time and on my own terms, and for a Spanish-language album, the numbers were actually quite good. Afterward I came back to the studio to continue recording the album in English, which I had stopped working on halfway through. I had learned my lesson: I would never again go on tour while recording an album at the same time. It is unnecessary madness, and I'll never do it again.

The name of the album in English was eventually *Life*, and the album was released in 2005. Even though it is without a doubt an interesting record that has a lot of influences and sounds, I have to admit that it isn't my favorite album of all the ones I've made. I wanted to make an introspective, contemplative, and multifaceted record, just like life. I wanted to connect with my emotions. I think I did accomplish this, at least to a certain extent. But that album ended up being influenced by many different cultures, and some of the criticism was that although each song was good on its own, the album as a whole was lacking in coherence.

My answer was always, "That's just how life is," since every phase or period of one's life is different. In that sense, I am not the same person I was one hour ago, or the same person I was yesterday or this morning. And that is exactly what makes life so interesting. But with all that said, I know the critics were right; the production was scattered, and in large part I attribute that to the fact that we released the album a full five years after we began recording it. If you start to work on something now, in five years you'll probably realize that many things have happened to you. You have new emotions, new life experiences—and then there's the new technology! It can be a computer or a change in the manufacture of an instrument, but technology creates a whole new series of sounds and influences. And all that affects the final product.

Regardless, the album we released was of impeccable quality. When I stop and think about why it took me so long to record it, I believe it was because I was hiding. To a certain degree, I think I was still hurt by everything that happened with "Livin' La Vida Loca," the sheer exhaustion that I reached and the intensity of the whole experience. It was almost like having a broken heart after being madly in love. I still loved the stage and the way I felt when I stood in front of an audience, but deep down I feared that what happened before might happen again. In a way I wanted to be there, but then again, I didn't. Not at all.

It took me some time before I was ready to face the world again. But the time I spent out of the public eye was one of the most important periods of my life. I learned a lesson in humility: For a long time I saw myself as some kind of superman who was held back by nothing. I learned what my limits were, and even more important, I learned how to tell others what my limits are. I would no longer do *everything* that was asked of me; I could no longer be everywhere at once. I didn't even want to. I learned to love my life again, and most of all I reconnected with the person I used to be. I realized that everything I had lived through those last few years had been without a doubt a dream—but along the way I had forgotten to be myself.

I learned that for me to be the master of my own life, I need to treat it with respect and responsibility. I need to be the one to decide what's best for me; I need to look for what I need when I need it, and not let anyone else dictate what I should or should not do. My life is *mine* and I control it. To this day, this is an intention I hold on to tightly, because if I don't look after my temple, or prevent others from invading it, then who will?

FIVE

THE SOUND
OF SILENCE

LIFE'S MOST VALUABLE LESSONS ARE LEARNED IN ABSOLUTE silence. It is when we are deep in that silence that we have the ability to think about and connect with our most intimate nature, our spiritual being. We all go through life—some in more of a rush than others—searching for happiness. It seems so simple, right? But we soon realize that before we find happiness, even before we begin to look for it, we need to understand what we are made of. We must connect with the little boy or girl we each have inside to discover our deepest dreams and the means to make them happen.

I have had the good fortune of having a great life. Extraordinary. But just as there are moments when I have felt I was at my peak, there have been others when I felt I had sunk to my lowest, and when the craziness of "Livin' La Vida Loca" came to an end, I was going through one of those moments. I was very tired and very sad. I was in the mood for nothing, and even though to the outside world it seemed I had everything, nothing material seemed to make a difference to me. The only thing I wanted was to stay home and do nothing. I had reached the upper echelons of the music industry—something for which I had worked tirelessly—

but now I was fed up and had no interest in using that power. The truth is I was simply exhausted, worn-out, and I didn't want to do a thing. So I isolated myself as much as I could.

What I didn't realize at the time was that I was really on the brink of so many extraordinary things that were about to come my way. Even though I felt I had lost hope, everything in my life was aligning to bring me to this exact point of desperation in order to incite me to ask questions and find answers I would have never imagined. The thing I realized later is that I spent way too much time looking outward, as opposed to inward. I made decisions either purely based on what my mind told me—mechanically— or purely based on what I felt with my heart—passionately. Individually, both ways of handling life are incorrect, and what I needed was to find the balance between the two. I needed to find my center. I needed to go deep down to find those forgotten emotions, covered and sabotaged by the adrenaline and the euphoria I had lived through over the last few years.

After going through so much and having so much, what I wanted now was the polar opposite: I wanted to find absolute simplicity. As always, life sent me exactly what I needed when I needed it the most.

THE LITTLE YOGI

At the end of 1998, when I was in the middle of all the chaos of *"La Copa de la Vida"* and the preparation for my first English album, I gave a concert in Bangkok. We went from one place to another with very little extra time, which was our usual pace. At one point, after giving a press conference, I went through the kitchen of a hotel to get back up to my room unnoticed, and suddenly, in the midst of all the chaos in the kitchen, I saw a man who had a very special aura. He looked like a small Gandhi. Normally, I would have walked right by him, but there was something about him that grabbed my attention.

"Hello," I said in English.

And he replied in Spanish: *"Hola!"*

"Hola?" I said. "You speak Spanish?"

"Of course," he said. "I'm Puerto Rican, too."

"Are you here on vacation?" I asked him, surprised.

Around us, chefs and plates came and went along with large dishes piled high with food. The security guards were waiting for me at the elevator bank so I could quickly return to my room to eat and rest a bit before the show. But at that particular moment I felt that time was frozen. The man emanated such a high level of peace and serenity that it was as if nothing else existed around us.

"No, no," he responded, "I am Puerto Rican but I have lived in Bangkok for the past eighteen years."

He told me that he used to be a Buddhist monk and that he had lived in India. As a monk he had traveled to Nepal and Tibet, and he later spent many years in the mountains of Thailand. But one day he fell in love with a Chinese woman and decided to stop being a monk so that he could get married and start a family. Now he worked at the hotel.

"Monkeys are born monkeys because they are meant to live up in the trees," he said, "and human beings are born to reproduce. So I stopped being a monk, and now I am married and have two beautiful daughters. Even though I am no longer a monk, the experience helped me find my way."

His words touched my soul. His story intrigued me as well as his wisdom, but most of all I felt something special in the presence of this man and I didn't want him to leave so fast. I wanted to keep asking him questions, and to hear the rest of his story. I don't know if it was because he was Puerto Rican like me, or if it was because he had such a special aura, but I felt that we had a very powerful connection. Maybe it was just intuition, but the fact is I wasn't wrong.

"Wait a minute!" I said to him. "You and I have to talk. Do you have a moment to come with me? I would love to speak with you some more."

He answered with a great big smile and came up in the elevator with me, to my room. Once there, we continued our conversation.

Recently I had begun to realize that there was a whole world of spiritual disciplines that until now I had ignored. A friend of mine, who was then one of my backup singers, was very immersed in the subject of esotericism, and he was slowly introducing me to this world. At that point it was enough for someone to say the word "yoga" or "karma" or "meditation," and I was fascinated.

"This is so amazing. Right now, I am interested in these very subjects, and you show up in my world at this exact moment," I said to the ex-monk.

After sitting there together for a while, I called my friend the backup singer to come and join us. And the three of us began to talk about life. We talked about so many things that I no longer remember any of the details, but I know they had a huge impact on me. By the time we were called for the sound check, my head was spinning. I asked my new friend to stay with us while we did the sound check, and once again, he accepted.

I was so fascinated with the conversation I was having with my friend and the ex-monk that I tried to absorb each word they said and every concept they explained. Even though I knew a bit about the philosophy they were discussing, the depths of what they were talking about were completely new to me. As they were talking, it became time for dinner and some food was brought up from the kitchen. I asked the ex-monk: "You're not going to eat?"

"Don't worry about it," he said to me. "This is nourishment for me. I feel satisfaction just from sitting here talking and sharing with you."

I mention this as one of the many wise reflections this man gave me that day. He is an extraordinary man who opened my eyes to a whole new world I had no previous knowledge of, and he taught me what I needed to do in order to learn more.

As we got to know one another even better, the spiritual connection I felt with him from the beginning turned out to be very real. I felt as though we had known each other all of our lives. Just as it is said that there is love at first sight, our friendship was like friendship at first sight. Today I refer to him as the little yogi, not because he holds the official title of "yogi" within the yoga practice, but simply to give him the name of some kind of teacher, considering how much he has taught me. He became a spiritual guide for me.

I feel that for most of my life I have been on a spiritual journey. I have always sought to find tranquillity, serenity, inner peace, God—regardless of the name that is given to Him/Her. So when I encountered this man who emanated so much wisdom and such a deep understanding of these subjects, it did not take long to convince me that the three of us (myself, my backup singer, and our new friend) would need to go on a journey to the source of his knowledge.

OPENING MY WESTERN EYES

EIGHT DAYS AFTER meeting the little yogi in Bangkok, I flew back home to Miami for the opening of a restaurant. But we didn't say good-bye for too long, as the decision had already been made: We planned to travel to India together; all I had to do was take care of some pending matters before we would embark on our expedition. First and foremost, what excited me the most was the chance to take some time off to backpack through India. I had never had the chance to do anything like this. For the first time in a long time, I was excited about the prospect of a trip, but what I didn't know was that this trip would be so radically different from all the trips I had ever taken.

I landed in Miami in the morning, and that very night at seven in the evening we held the opening of the restaurant for the public and the press. Just three hours later, at ten o'clock at night, I boarded a plane once again, this time en route to India. Had it been a work thing, I would have probably not been as excited, but this time it was different; I felt a kind of special energy. As we had planned, my friend the backup singer came along with me, and together we arrived in Calcutta to meet our new friend.

I had been to India a couple of times, but they were always work trips and always for very short periods of time. Even though it's a country that had always intrigued and fascinated me, I had never had the time to properly explore it. Every time I would visit a city for the first time, I'd try my best to see as many of the main attractions as possible, but it was never enough to give me a real sense of the place or the people.

There was something about India that deeply intrigued me and drew me in, and I had always wanted to see more of it. As a country, India already occupied a special place in my heart, but it was not until I went there with my friend the ex-monk that I realized how little of it I really knew. It was not until I arrived with my backpack slung over my shoulder to meet my spiritual leader that I could finally discover the true beauty of Mother India.

The little yogi had it all planned out. We'd spend the first night in Calcutta, and then we would travel to the small village of Puri by train.

I always say that whoever goes to India and does not visit a train station has not really been to India. Indian train stations are some of the most amazing places I have ever seen, full of people, activities, sounds, smells, and colors. The important thing is to forget that you are a foreigner, to see yourself as part of the snapshot and reality of that moment. Because if not, the chaos that can ensue is enough to make a person go running in the other direction. Hundreds of people hustle and bustle to get a spot on the train. People scream and argue, and all you want to do is get to your seat with your backpack. Children on the street run all along the sides of the train, screaming: "Hello! Hello, sir!"

The day we went to take the train to Puri, in the midst of all the mayhem, there were four kids who yanked at my backpack and pulled on my pant legs. I told them no several times, until I finally took off my backpack and said, "Stop!"

They were speaking Bengali. And I spoke to them in Spanish and English. But they spoke neither, and I, of course, didn't speak Bengali.

So, I took hold of the four kids and said to them, "Hold on!" and I began to sing: *"Palo, palo, palo, palo, palito, palo es . . ."*

It's a typical Latin American children's song, the kind you teach very young children.

They were mesmerized. "Eh?" they said with a surprised look on their faces. But soon enough they started imitating the words to the song.

"Palo, palo, palo, palo, palito, palo es . . . ," they repeated.

Just then and totally unexpectedly, I taught those children something that came from my part of the world. Once again, music transcended the language barriers that would have otherwise come between us. And even though they didn't understand a word of what I was saying, I felt that we made a connection through music. It was a singular moment, in which we lessened the gap between our cultures and touched something very deep within our humanity.

After playing with the kids for a little while, I finally said good-bye to them and boarded the train amid all the madness and we headed toward Puri.

Puri is a well-known town because one of the most sacred temples of Hindu culture is situated there. The temple, which has existed for thousands of years, is called Shree Jagannath, as it is dedicated to the Hindu god Jagganatha, which is an incarnation of Krishna. Only Hindus are allowed to enter the temple. Each year, thousands of Vishne-Krishna worshippers arrive at its doors, for a festival where they mount an idol of Krishna on a giant carriage that is carried all through the streets of Puri.

The city is also known as the Golden Beach, due to the golden sands of the beaches that face the Bay of Bengal. It is a place with unique views, where you can watch the sunrise and sunset from the same place, without moving, and where at sunset you can gaze directly at the sun without burning your eyes.

In addition to all of this, Puri is a spiritual retreat for yoga and is the center of many religions. There are many *mathas* (Hindu monasteries) of the various branches of Hinduism, as well as Christian, Jewish, and Muslim houses of prayer. It is impressive to see how all these religions can coexist. They all share this extraordinary little village, and each one has its own temple, where they can practice their religion in peace and absolute tranquillity. The town is also a sacred place where people come to die and to be cremated.

In one day alone, I saw the cremation of a Muslim; a Hindu ceremony that involves throwing the body into the river; and a Buddhist, a Christian, and a Hindu sharing tea in a small bar: the Buddhist monk had a *mala* on his wrist, the Christian had a cross hanging down his chest, and the Hindu had a *tilaka* on his forehead. I couldn't believe it. It was such an extraordinary vision that my head started to spin. How can it be that in the Western world we are so limited?

We come from a society that tells us that just because of their religion, people are good or bad. We load ourselves up with prejudices and cultural stigmas that are based on what? On nothing. We have been taught to fear anyone who is different from us. . . . Why? Because of sheer ignorance. Instead of focusing on the differences that exist between human beings, we should instead focus on the similarities—and the fact is there are so many! That's what I do from a spiritual point of view as well as in my everyday life. I always seek to find a common denominator, and the truth is that I almost always find one. There are millions of cultures in the world, right? We are all different in so many ways, but ultimately what matters is that we are all human beings. The only thing we really need to live is the urge to breathe. And when we get cut, the blood that comes out of our bodies is the same color.

The only thing I desire in my life, and in the lives of all other human beings, is to find inner peace. It doesn't matter what path you choose to reach it. Be it Catholicism, Islam, Buddhism, Hinduism, Christianity, Judaism, quantum physics, Taoism, atheism—what matters is to find what works for each of us, and since each one of our minds is a universe on its own, it's not surprising that each of us would need to find a different way to reach his own state of inner peace. No one thing is better than another; no one religion is more effective or more valid than another. The key is to find one's own way. In Buddhism there is a teaching that says the worst thing you can do to your spirit is tell someone his faith is wrong. Not only is it an act of extreme arrogance toward others—it is also the worst thing you can do to your own karma. This is a very powerful concept that, if we all apply it, can make the world a better place.

For me, one of the greatest failures of human beings is that we always search for a way to define people, to categorize them and give them a label. And within these categories that are created by man, there are, of course, good and bad things. To not categorize them as either positive or negative when we call them "good" or "bad," I instead try to visualize them as frequencies that are either compatible or incompatible with mine. I have simply decided to grab on to the compatible ones, those that help me and nourish my spirit, and I try not to focus on whatever steals my peace or decelerates the growth of my soul. I always seek whatever is most effective for me, what aligns most closely with my own personal beliefs, religion, or philosophy. I try to remain open to everything and I make a concerted effort to always find new teachings and new paths everywhere I go and in every situation I find myself in. If I limited myself to being only a Buddhist or a Catholic or a Hindu, to a certain degree I would be closing myself off from receiving other lessons from other beliefs and philosophies. I had some wonderful experiences with Catholicism and I also have a strong affinity to certain Buddhist teachings. In fact, I see many similarities between Hinduism and Christianity, and I feel that in each one I find answers to the challenges I face in my personal life.

There is a story in Sanskrit that says Jesus—during the so-called lost years, in which, according to the Bible, he disappeared and went to meditate—traveled all over India and crossed the Himalayas to get to Tibet. It is said that he joined up with a caravan and traveled throughout the Middle East (crossing through Iraq, Iran, Afghanistan, and Pakistan) until he arrived in India, Nepal, and later Tibet. There are dozen of facts that support this affirmation, but the most interesting one to me is that upon returning from his trip, Jesus washed the feet of his disciples. Isn't that curious? Jesus explained to his apostles that washing the feet of a fellow human being is a sign of humility and servitude. In fact, the custom exists in other religions, such as Islam and Sikhism, and in Hinduism touching the feet of another person is a sign of respect. I don't think something like this can be a coincidence. To me that piece of information has a reason, and it crystallizes the connection I myself feel exists among all religions.

THE SWAMI

In Puri the little yogi took us to an ashram—a place of meditation—where we spent time studying yoga and sharing with the Swami Yogeshwarananda Giri, a master sage who had reached a very high level in the practice of yoga.

The swami was a very quiet man who radiated a very special light, a beautiful energy. I had the honor of meeting him, because at one point in his life the little Puerto Rican yogi had lived in that ashram and studied with Yogeshwarananda Giri's master, who was called Paramahamsa Hariharananda. Just as the swami himself had studied under the tutelage of some other great master, now another student—the little yogi—was bringing him a new generation of students—us. Before that swami there had been another swami, and another one before him; it's beautiful to think there is a long line of masters and students to which I was now having access. But it is important to clarify that just because I was a student of the swami does not mean I can teach the techniques that he taught me, as I am not trained to do so. The swami was born to be a yogi: He spent his entire life studying and preparing his body to be a yogi, and that is his destiny. I, on the other hand, only had the privilege to study with him for a short period.

The first time I met the Swami Yogeshwarananda, I noted that the little yogi—his disciple—did not kiss his feet, but he did touch them and recited a prayer. I saw his gesture as a beautiful demonstration of humility and respect. So I did as my friend and kneeled down to touch the man's feet. Because I didn't know what one is supposed to say or think while touching the swami's feet, I started to recite the Lord's Prayer. I think it was the quickest "Our Father" I have ever prayed in my life, because I found it strange to remain kneeling in front of the master for so long. It was a totally new situation for me and I did not know what to do. So many things crossed my mind, including, "What would my buddies say if they saw me do this?" I could even imagine my manager's face, as he tried to stop people from taking photos of the scene that could end up in something like *People* magazine.

Inside I was laughing, but later I realized that this small act of humility represented so much. I had spent so many years living in a world of glamour, luxury travel, hotel suites, and private planes that that simple act of humility was something I profoundly needed. Getting down on my knees and touching the dirty feet of another man was a very symbolic and powerful gesture for me, because it meant casting my ego aside as well as the aggrandized image I had of myself because of everything I had accomplished. I could have very easily just shaken the man's hand and said: "Good afternoon, how are you?" But no. I kneeled down on the floor and touched his feet, and from that moment I felt something vibrate within. I felt I was doing the right thing, and that is how I began the long road back to connecting with the deepest part of my being. I had spent too many years separating my public person from my private one, and I was finally starting to find the way to reconcile those two polar opposite sides of my existence.

With the swami I studied kriya yoga, a very passive type of yoga that has a lot to do with reflection. It isn't a kind of yoga that requires a lot of physical exertion, but is instead a process of internal exploration. It was through this process that the swami helped me open the so-called kundalini—an evolutionary energy, invisible and immeasurable, that ascends through the spine, moving through the seven chakras of being. It's pretty crazy, because supposedly through the practice of kriya yoga one will ultimately begin to hear the body's natural sounds. According to the philosophy of kriya yoga, the body is full of sounds and fluids where energy comes and goes; what happens is that we, in our mad rush to live in the modern world, ignore them. But these bodily sounds are what they really call the sound of silence, which, once you hear it, can connect you with your own center, where you will find tranquillity, serenity, and peace.

Silence is really one single note, just one note. It is the sound you hear when you turn off all the lights and all the gadgets in your house, when you are alone and you lie down in your bed to sleep. What you hear in those moments is the sound of silence. And it is the sound that one seeks to hear through the practice. That is the note I am looking for in my meditation, the one that allows me to concentrate and removes me from everything around me. That is what the swami taught me.

When I arrived at this ashram, in that village by the sea in a corner of India, I didn't know anything about this. I had traveled to India because I thought it was an interesting country, because I needed to rest, because the little yogi's words awoke a curiosity in me. But I didn't have the slightest clue what I was looking for. I didn't imagine what I would learn. In fact, my vision was so simple that when I was told that the swami was a yoga master, I imagined he would teach me how to stretch or touch my big toe to my ear.

As we know it in the West, the practice of yoga has been completely commercialized. Today it is just another business, and anyone can become a yoga instructor just by paying several hundred dollars to become certified. But in India, the country where yoga was born, the people who teach it have spent entire lifetimes preparing to do so. Now, I am not saying that commercial yoga is a bad thing—if it works for you and gives you the peace and tranquillity you need, then carry right along. But because I had the good fortune to be able to learn from a sage who explained the whole philosophy on which it is based, this is the yoga that I practice.

I only spent four days with the swami on that trip, but those four days changed my life completely. Every day we would do a ceremony in which he would repeat various Sanskrit mantras with the purpose of helping me to find that divine sound, the sound of silence. Once you find the sound of silence and you are able to hear it in any situation, be it in a train station when you are surrounded by lots of people or alone in your room, you get closer to seeing the divine pendulum and feeling a divine vibration. The divine pendulum is something we always carry within; it is a frequency that moves from ear to ear when we close our eyes. Only through practice will you be able to appreciate this. And later, with more practice, you are able to feel the divine vibration that circulates throughout your whole body.

Everything begins with silence. Once you find the sound of silence, you are able to separate yourself from all that is physical and everything around you. That's when you can advance to the next level—the divine vibration and the pendulum.

When he taught me this I not only believed that I found my center, but I also connected with the energy of the universe. He sat down next to me and placed his hand on my ears and I heard it right away—that high note that came from deep within me. Later the swami placed one hand on my spine and the other hand on my chest and asked: "Do you feel it?"

And in that precise moment, I felt the vibration. Later he put his hands on my eyes and I could see the pendulum, exactly as he had described it to me.

I thought, "What is this? This man is a magician!"

Later I tried to do it again on my own, but I couldn't. So he said to me:

"Keep trying. Keep meditating, because with practice you will get there. With practice everything is possible. When the end comes, everyone will throw themselves to the ground and pray. When the chaos comes, when the world is coming to an end with tsunamis, hurricanes, and tornadoes, the people will all gather together and start to pray. That will be their way of facing what lies ahead. But you . . . you are going to sit and find the sound of silence. You will feel the divine vibration in your body and you will see the pendulum. The world may be crumbling around you, but you will be focused and in peace."

Never again did I feel what I experienced with the swami, maybe for lack of practice, but what did remain vibrating inside me was his profound teaching. Applying what I learned on that trip, I feel that the real significance of his words was that it doesn't matter how much noise or how many people may be around you; if you are balanced and in peace you can be sitting and talking with someone and still find the sound of silence. If you allow it, a police car can be passing right by you with the siren wailing at maximum volume, and you won't even hear it. A plane can land on the roof of your house and you won't even notice. That is the power of the sound of silence. As you hear it, you can disconnect from your body and at once connect with your soul.

Before going to India, I seldom spent time alone or in silence. When I walked into a room I would turn on the television right away, but not to watch it, just to have some company. The noise, the sounds, anesthetized me, and this way I kept myself far away from whatever was going on inside, as I was scared to see the ugly things I might discover. But when I returned from India, I began to search for the opposite. I wanted silence. I *needed* silence. Every morning I would spend thirty-five minutes to an hour practicing yoga and meditation, and I'd do the same in the afternoons. Those moments became a sacred portion of my day, and knowing that I had them helped me to feel calmer when I was in the midst of all the chaos. They taught me to face myself, so that I could begin to destroy, one by one, the very fears that made me escape from my own truth.

Unfortunately, when I had been home for a while, I went back to my old routines. If I normally gave myself thirty minutes to an hour to meditate, slowly that turned into twenty, then ten, until I stopped meditating altogether. Could it be that those moments in silence brought me too close to my truth, the truth that I would sooner or later have to face? Maybe. But if anything is obvious, it is that it still was not my time.

THREE LITTLE GIRLS

MY SECOND ENCOUNTER with the magical teachings of India came at the end of 2000. I had been working incessantly for two years: Since my last trip to India, I'd had the Grammy Awards, the release of *Ricky Martin* (in English), the success that came from "Livin' La Vida Loca," the recording of *Sound Loaded*, and all of the promotional work for that second album in English. Now I was in the midst of my time off, not really knowing what it was I wanted to do next.

Once again, I didn't have much time to think about the matter because destiny had already mapped out my next step. One day while I was at home—one of those days when I was feeling particularly sad and listless—I got a call from a colleague who was living in India.

"Ricky, I want you to see what I am doing in Calcutta," he said to me. "I have started an orphanage for girls."

During those days I wasn't in the mood for anything. All I wanted was to stay locked up at home in my pajamas, watching films, listening to music, and sleeping. Today I realize how badly I was really doing; I see photographs taken of me during that period and I almost don't recognize myself. My eyes are glassy—they look completely empty—and my smile looks completely fake.

However, the prospect of going to India gave me a jolt. I don't know—maybe it was because of the deep sense of peace I had felt there before, or because I was starting to connect with myself, but something inside me made me say, "You have to do this." It was almost as if, on some organic level, I knew what awaited me there.

"Wonderful!" I said to him with a renewed sense of enthusiasm. "I'm coming!"

Within days I was boarding a plane to Calcutta. I arrived in India, but this time I was not remotely ready to find what I discovered.

The orphanage was a stunning place, beautifully painted and decorated, and it had plenty of room to play and study. There was a music school and a primary and secondary school; and they offered cooking classes for those who didn't want to study. . . . The place was a dream. When I finished my tour, I said to my friend, "What you have here is a Disney World for girls!"

My friend founded a fantastic institution that offers care and education to helpless girls in Calcutta. The work he has done there is incredible and completely inspiring. He is dedicated to rescuing girls from the most dangerous streets in the city and offers them a place to live, an alternative to their way of life.

My friend didn't care that I had just arrived, that I might be tired and have a case of jet lag: He immediately asked if I wanted to come with him to go rescue more girls from the street. And even though I didn't really understand how we were going to do it, I of course accepted.

We set out to explore the streets. We went to all the corners of Calcutta's poorest neighborhoods, and we walked through long and dirty streets, moving through the throngs, looking for abandoned girls, or worse. It was shocking to see the places where they tend to live. In the slums of Calcutta, four branches and a piece of plastic are a house, and you are lucky if you have the piece of plastic to shelter you from the rain. Many people don't. I asked my friend, "Why do you only rescue girls? Why does the center only have girls, and not boys? Don't boys need help, too?"

"For better or worse, the boys of Calcutta survive," my friend explained to me. "They beg or work or figure out a way to survive one way or another. The girls are also strong and resourceful, but they are often forced into prostitution, which is what I am trying to avoid."

"But how can it be?" I asked him. "We're talking about girls who are no more than four or six years old. . . . How can it be?"

"Unfortunately, that's how it is," he responded. "It's horrible, but the reality is that it happens all the time. There are men who are willing to pay in order to rape a four-year-old girl."

He didn't have to say another word.

We combed those neighborhoods until we found a group of beggars, exactly the type of girls who were at risk of falling into child prostitution. There were three girls and their mother. They lived under a plastic bag that was nailed to a concrete wall, and the other side was tied to a tree. It was raining and there, under that tiny improvised roof, were the mother and her three daughters, one of whom was very ill. There was no time to lose. With the help of a boy who translated everything into Bengali, we explained the situation to the mother: why we believed that her daughters were at risk, what might happen, and the alternative we could offer through the foundation. She understood and agreed, so we took the mother and the three daughters with us—including the one who was sick—and we quickly rushed them back to my hotel.

But when we arrived, people looked at us with disgusted looks on their faces. Of course, it was an elegant hotel and it bothered them to see at least ten Westerners walk into this refined atmosphere with a group of beggars. But I was so worried about them that I didn't care about the stares as I walked in holding two girls in my arms, with the mother behind me carrying the little girl who was sick. A girl who also worked as a volunteer at the orphanage, and who later became a very close friend, said to them, "They are my guests," and that would have to do.

The hotel staff obviously did not like it at all that I was taking them to my room, but I think that because of a mixture of hospitality and respect, their only option was to let me do as I pleased. Upon arriving at my room, we called for the hotel doctor, who came up right away. But when the man entered my room and saw who his patients were, he said, "Dear Lord! What is this?"

"Well," I said, "these are three girls and their mother, and one of them needs your help—she is very sick."

The three girls were all bitten up by rats. The two older ones were dirty and very thin, but they were in relatively good shape. However, the little one, who was approximately four or five years old, looked like she was on the brink of death. Her eyes would roll back and she was as limp as a rag doll.

I looked at the doctor.

"We have to give the little one something," I said to him. "I don't know what she has, but please do something."

The doctor wouldn't even get close to the little girl.

"Okay," he said, pointing at a nearby napkin, "please take that rag and clean her up."

"But, sir!" I said to him. "If it was a matter of cleaning her up, I would have done so myself a long time ago. What I need is for you to examine her and tell me what she has. I need you to check her eyes, her ears, her temperature . . . whatever you have to do to tell me if she is ill or if it's an infection—just tell me what it is!"

But he still wouldn't touch her.

"It's just that I don't know . . . ," he said.

"Look!" I said, this time more firmly. "I have antibiotics that I brought with me from the United States. I can give them to her. But I am not a doctor, and I need you to tell me what it is that she needs!"

"I don't know . . . ," this man who called himself a doctor kept saying.

I couldn't take it anymore and I said, "You know what? We don't need you. Please leave." He turned and left shamelessly. He simply grabbed his things and rushed out the door, thanking me as he left.

I couldn't believe it. I had always believed that a doctor's duty was to save lives, all lives that needed saving, but this "doctor" was apparently only a doctor to those he felt like being a doctor to. According to the caste system in India, those girls and their mother are labeled "untouchables" (the lowest caste), and even in a life-or-death situation, that doctor was not going to touch them. The hierarchy of the castes is a concept that is deeply entrenched in Indian culture and has a reason for being, despite the fact that I cannot understand it. That's how it is. I am not judging it in any way. It's just that because of the way I was raised, and the many things I have seen in this world, I just can't comprehend it.

We managed to get through the night, and early the next morning the doctor from the orphanage center arrived and he, of course, had no problem examining her. He looked at her eyes, he took her pulse, and after checking her thoroughly, he said, "The only thing this girl has is a stomach virus."

"How can that be?" I asked, surprised. Most of us get sick when we eat a piece of chicken that hasn't been cooked through, or poorly washed seafood, but these girls . . . these girls were born on the street and ate anything that crossed their path. Their bellies had to be made of iron! God knows what she must have eaten to become so ill!

"I'm telling you," he replied. "All she has to do is take this medicine and in a few hours she will be just fine."

So she took the medication, and within two hours that little girl was running from one side of the room to the other, climbing all over me. She grabbed the television's remote control and kept asking what everything was.

That day they slept in my friend's hotel room. The next day we took the three girls and their mother to the orphanage, which isn't in Calcutta proper, but instead about an hour's drive outside the city. It was beautiful, because when we arrived, the rest of the girls came out to welcome us. They all looked so pretty, dressed in their uniforms with garlands of flowers around their necks. They also placed garlands around the necks of those of us who had just arrived.

To this day, those three girls live in that center, where they are very happy. Later on, they were joined by their older sister, who had run away at the exact moment we'd picked the girls up. She was afraid because she didn't know what our intentions were, but once she came to visit her sisters with her mother, and saw how well the girls were doing, she decided to stay there as well.

The mother, however, went back to the streets. A Spanish woman who had heard about the situation gave her an apartment in order to get her off the streets, but after just one week of living there she decided to return to her corner, where she could beg. "I am happy here," she said. "This is what I know. Leave me here. I don't need anything else."

And even though she is in the streets, she is nevertheless an amazing mother. She visits her daughters on the weekends and maintains a relationship with them. Although they live apart, she seems happy to see that her daughters are living under better conditions than the ones she had to offer them.

Today I am the three youngest girls' sponsor, so I have been able to contribute to making their lives a little better. They are happy, but what they don't know is that they have given me so much more than I could ever give them. They give me strength, they give me hope, and they make me see what is truly beautiful in life, because they have taught me that the only thing one really requires to live is the urge to breathe.

Everything in life arrives at its moment. Those girls came into my life at the time when I most needed them, to ground me and show me a touch of simplicity. They forced me to reassess my priorities and they showed me that true beauty in life usually exists in the simplest of things. They appeared at a time in my life when I wanted to please my record label, the members of my band, my family, my friends . . . but what I didn't realize was that by trying to please everyone else, I was betraying myself, because I was not thinking about myself, about what I really needed to be happy. I believed that my happiness consisted of pleasing others, and that ruined me for a long time. With the girls I learned that happiness really appears at the times when one is finally able to detach from all those types of complications.

They would say to me, "Come and sit on the floor. We're going to play." They had only three pebbles, and that's what we played with. So how is it that we need all of these things—computers, video games, televisions, sound systems, cars—to have a good time? These girls taught me that if my clothes are ironed, it's fine, and that if they're not, that's fine as well. Most of the things we often consider "important" really aren't that important in the big scheme of things. Life is as simple or as complicated as we make it.

After I met the girls and discovered the simplicity with which they lived and the innocence they carried in their souls despite the hard lives they had lived, I felt an immense desire to reconnect with Kiki, that boy I abandoned when I got on a plane on that rainy day in San Juan. There is something so beautiful in the innocence of youth, and it breaks my heart to know that there are so many children out there who are stripped of their basic right to just be kids.

FINDING BALANCE

WHEN I LOOK back, I realize that those trips to India marked me in a very profound way. One might think it was all a big coincidence that I went through both of these experiences in this extraordinary country, but deep in my heart I know it is not the case. I know that the cosmos sent me these lessons because that is how it had to be, and because there is something in that country, with its colors, its people, and its energy, that vibrates with the same frequency as my soul.

Everything I ask of the cosmos comes when it is meant to come. It took me a while to understand this, but now that I know it and have integrated it into my own philosophy, I live a much more peaceful life. Instead of worrying about what might be or what could have been, I stay focused on the present and on what I need to do to reach my own happiness, because whatever it is I may be lacking, I know the cosmos will ultimately send my way.

It was thanks to the silence I found through the teachings of my swami that I could for the first time look at myself in the mirror and see who was really standing there. In the peace and tranquillity of the ashram, the daily rituals of cleaning, cooking, and meditation, I found the bubble of silence that I needed to reconnect with the boy I once was. I could open myself to the universe to hear what it was telling me, and what I found was a world of beauty and transparency. From that moment on, I found the equilibrium I so longed for, and for the first time I understood that what I want most out of life is to give—and to give in this very concrete manner—because ultimately, it is the very best way to receive.

In India I found what I consider to be the three keys of life: serenity, simplicity, and spirituality. I was able to comprehend the enormous blessing that is my life, and I discovered that true wealth does not exist outside, but instead lives inside of me. From that moment on, gratitude became a huge part of my life, and instead of hiding all the things that caused me pain and discomfort, I started to look at them head-on, without fear.

SIX

THE ROLE
OF MY LIFE

I'M SURE I'M NOT ALONE, BUT I SPEND A LOT OF TIME searching for my life's purpose. Of course, I want to have the kind of work I am passionate about, a family that loves me, and friends who support me . . . but deep down, beneath all of those things that are more like needs than anything else, lives my desire to contribute to the world in a profound and lasting way. Ultimately, my presence on this earth will only last a short time (relatively speaking), and the desire to leave a mark is a very natural thing.

For a long time I thought my way of contributing to the world, of showing gratitude for all the miracles and favors received, was through music. When I get up to sing onstage in front of thousands of people, I feel a very human and powerful vibration. Music allows me to connect with the audience at a visceral level, and through music I feel that I transmit my entire essence, my very being. It is a unique privilege to be able to feel what I feel when I'm up there, and this sentiment has always made me believe that this was my mission: to convey joy, rhythm, and movement to others.

But after my last trip to India I began to realize performing onstage was simply not enough. Even though being onstage gave me immense satisfaction, it is a satisfaction that only really serves me. The three girls, and my experiences in their country, made me realize what I was really missing.

FINDING MY CAUSE

I WAS AT a point in my life when I was questioning everything. The feeling of helping these girls had been so powerful that I no longer knew if music was really my mission, or if it had simply been a tool that helped me find the path to philanthropy and helping the most defenseless among us. I came back from India thinking deeply about what my friend told me, and how those three girls could have easily fallen into human trafficking. When I returned home, I spent three days sleeping because of how drained I felt after everything I had seen. The experience with the three girls shook me so profoundly, and I was still not sure how I was going to fit this newly gained awareness into the rest of my life. I knew I didn't want to go on with my life as before, and that I had to do something; I just didn't know what it was.

When I finally got out of bed, after resting for what felt like an eternity, I began to investigate. I went online and started to read everything I could about human trafficking. I realized that this was not only a problem in India, and that it is actually an epidemic that affects the whole world. I realized that in reality it isn't necessarily a question of wealth or poverty, but that it is actually an issue of values, of human rights—which makes it all the more tragic. As long as there are people who want to continue believing that boys or girls should be exploited for the simple reason that they are young and defenseless, this type of crime will continue to exist.

My reading awoke a lot of rage, anger, and frustration within me. I learned that each year more than 1 million children become victims of trafficking. Do you know what that means, more than 1 million children every year? That means that every day, almost three thousand kids are kidnapped, sold, abused, and God knows what else. And most are girls. There are men who are willing to pay $15,000 for the virginity of an eight-year-old girl. The fact that there are men out there who think this way is incomprehensible, and in my opinion anyone who allows this to happen and to keep happening deserves to be imprisoned.

After doing all this research, realizing everything that was at stake, and seeing what can be done, I went to Washington, D.C., and met people who to this day are my mentors in the fight against human trafficking. They taught me everything I needed to know to help me further this fight in a tangible way, and have guided me so that I could help in the most effective way possible.

And that's how I began working for the cause. I think there was a bit of selfishness in my desire to help, because I did it in large part to relieve myself of the pain I felt upon witnessing such a tragedy. I needed a form of catharsis, a way to do away with all the anguish, the rage, and the frustration I felt upon seeing what could have happened to my three girls and to the millions of children who suffer each day at the hands of abusive adults. It is an infuriating situation, because it somehow feels like you're swimming against the current. There is so much work to be done that anything I did wouldn't be more than a drop in the ocean. You might be able to rescue one child, but every day there are thousands more who continue to be forced into prostitution or to become sex slaves—this is the reality of modern slavery, and the saddest part about it is that it happens in cities all over the world.

So, what *can* be done?

When I took an interest in this cause, I knew it was not going to be easy. It's not that the situation was being ignored completely, because much has been discussed and written on the subject for many years. However, a true awareness of the gravity of what is really going on was lacking. The crime happens on various levels: The term "human trafficking" includes the factories that exploit their workers, prostitution, forced labor, sexual exploitation of minors, servitude, and organ trafficking. Within prostitution, there is child prostitution and child pornography. It is a pyramid with various levels.

The more I researched, the more I found. I educated myself on even the smallest details, which is how the People for Children project of the Ricky Martin Foundation came to be; through it, we defend children who are being exploited or who run the risk of exploitation. This project, which has been in effect for many years, was born from the rage I felt after what I saw, and all the people whom I met. It is my way of supporting the cause, although I know that the work we do will never be enough. I would like to be able to do so much more.

THE BIRTH OF MY FOUNDATION

PEOPLE FOR CHILDREN was actually an offshoot of a foundation that already existed, the Ricky Martin Foundation. The foundation was started to help disabled children in Puerto Rico, a project undertaken with the help of the Easter Seals/SER organization of Puerto Rico, through which a children's rehabilitation center was created. What happened was that Easter Seals/SER already had a rehabilitation center in San Juan, the capital. But there are children who live elsewhere on the island who could not get to this location because of distance. So we created a rehabilitation center in Aibonito, a town located in the center of the island, where people can easily come from farther away. Ever since its doors were opened, children have been able to receive treatment that was not previously available to them.

Later, when the foundation was up and running, we decided to broaden the spectrum of its functions to bring music to the children of Puerto Rico. And like so many things in my life, the project was born out of sheer happenstance. Or was it?

My niece, who at the time was attending art school, is a flute player, and she was showing me the flute her father had just bought for her. But while we were talking, she mentioned something that surprised me: She sometimes had to lend her flute to other kids in the class because they didn't have one. *What?!* I thought. An island like Puerto Rico, with its beautiful musical traditions, and the kids don't even have instruments! So I looked further into the matter, and informed myself more about musical education in the school system of my island, and I realized that it simply didn't exist. I called the Department of Education of Puerto Rico several times, and I discovered that at that time there was not one single desk that was focused on music, and if there was, they just didn't answer the phone. I don't know if things have changed since then, but I certainly hope so. Investigating a bit more, I realized that some schools did have music departments with classes and a few instruments, but generally the instruments were already used or in terrible condition, and they are usually scarce. Like in many parts of the world, there are never sufficient funds for education, much less for music.

The first thing we did was to form an alliance with Yamaha and FedEx to raise $1 million in musical instruments for the schools of Puerto Rico. Unfortunately, I couldn't participate in the delivery of the instruments, but my brothers and my friend Mireille Bravo, who were in charge of the whole program, organized it so that all the boxes of instruments were placed in the middle of the basketball court. It was a huge success, because the students would show up and say "Wow!" when they saw all the boxes. Even the students who were not enrolled in music signed up so they could have the chance to use the new instruments. The teachers couldn't believe it when they saw everything that arrived, and, on a personal level, I was happy to see that we were doing something for the future musicians of my island.

These were the first projects of the Ricky Martin Foundation, which since its inception has been an important part of my daily life. Today the foundation focuses on various fields—we can't do it all, but we do what we can, both locally and around the globe. One of the projects we're developing in Puerto Rico is a holistic youth center in Loiza, a town on the north coast of the island, where there are many gang-related problems. The idea is to build a place where we can keep these kids occupied and off the streets. The center will offer classrooms, but there will also be a place where we teach meditation, yoga, arts, and all kinds of other activities to keep them busy. I believe that one of the most serious problems faced by our society's youth is idleness. When they have too much free time on their hands, they have more opportunity to get into trouble, so our goal is to create a place where they will always be busy, a place that will be like an amusement park for children of all ages, from zero to eighteen years old. We also want to offer support to pregnant girls so they can deliver their babies in a healthy environment. The idea is to start healing these wounds that have opened within society, and help the gang members who are killing one another begin to realize their so-called enemies are kids just like them. In June 2009, the RTL Foundation of Germany selected our proposal for the construction of the Loiza center as their international project (along with four other European projects) and will support us with funds raised through their renowned telethon. It is a long-term project that will take a long time to implement, but we are doing it with a great deal of love.

From the moment we created the foundation, it was as if I had sent out the message to the universe that I wanted to do something, and so many ways of helping suddenly began to appear before me. All you have to do is say, "I want to do something," and *boom*, the opportunities start to crop up. It is really a question of selecting the causes that are most important to you personally or touch your heart in some way, because there is so much to do. I started with music and a rehabilitation center for kids with disabilities. Those covered the areas of health and education, two causes I consider very important. Social justice would come later on.

What I know is that giving back felt wonderful. Actually, it felt better than anything else I had done previously. And I know we could have done more at that time, but with the little we had done, I started to see very positive results, which filled me with joy. It was healing for the world, and healing for me to do it.

Even though I do devote as much of my time as possible to my foundation and we accomplish quite a lot, I still don't feel it's enough, and we're always looking for a way to do more. But sometimes things happen; in my case, I got a call from a colleague in India that led me to discover the horrible reality of human trafficking. No matter what the cause is that draws you, or inspires you to educate yourself further, hopefully the knowledge that it is almost impossible to eradicate issues such as these will inspire us all to do as much as we can, and then just a little bit more.

THE HORROR OF HUMAN TRAFFICKING

WHEN WE BEGAN to work on the issue of human trafficking, one of the obstacles we had to face is that it's such a colossal and brutal problem that it is often hard to get people to pay attention. It's like looking directly at a battlefield. It is so painful that people are inclined to turn their gaze elsewhere. That's what happened to me when I first saw it. I said, "What? There are people who buy and sell sex with a four-year-old child? This just can't be." But it is. And just because it is such a horrifying subject, we cannot cast it aside. It is instead the very reason why we should face it head-on, with our eyes wide-open, with the goal of bringing as much awareness to it as possible.

Like so many people, sometimes it happens that when I discover some of the atrocities that happen in the world, I feel like running in the opposite direction. I don't want to know what it is that's happening because I'm not ready to hear it. Like everyone, I also have my own problems, and it can be hard to think about what I can possibly do to help. But I have learned that the more I study, the more I know, and then I feel more prepared to face the reality of the situation and make my contribution toward finding a solution to the problem.

So, when I am seeking the support of others, I have learned that the best way to go about it is to ease them into the whole picture: I usually start by stating basic facts, gradually adding details, explaining, until they can finally grasp the full picture and ultimately understand it. Although on the one hand I am quite graphic in describing and explaining the issue, I have to be careful, because I don't want to intimidate potential supporters. On the contrary: What I want is for everyone to take a real interest in the subject. I am not going to paint a rose-colored picture of the situation just so people pay attention, but I will present it in the best way possible so that they understand it and aren't frightened away. I know I can't chase down politicians and citizens of the world and force them to listen to me, so it is crucial for me to know how I can reach them so that they do listen, and to convince them that if we all join forces, we can actually make a difference.

I want the world to understand that exploitation exists, that there are men and women who sell sexual servitude, the sexual services of a child, and that there are also people willing to pay for such services. In Cambodia, I met a fourteen-year-old girl who had been sold and raped. She was a beautiful girl. Her abductors told her, "If you come with us, we'll make you a model and the money you earn will be sent to your grandmother so that she will be able to get the medicine and therapies to treat her condition." Given that option, it goes without saying that the girl didn't hesitate to accept the offer. They were offering her an opportunity of a lifetime and, on top of that, a solution for her grandmother's illness. How could she say no? But the reality was, of course, very different. They kidnapped her and put her in a brothel, where a disgusting man raped her, got her pregnant, and gave her HIV. Had she not been found and taken to an orphanage where she and her baby would receive care, what would have become of her?

The worst part is that she is not the only one. There are millions of children with similar stories. I met a girl who had been sold to traffickers by her own father, to be able to feed the rest of his children; she was already infected with the AIDS virus and was the mother of a three-month-old baby. When I met her, she didn't know if the baby was also infected, because back then it took a few months to be able to tell if a baby was born with HIV or not.

I've heard hundreds of similar stories. The government tries to fight back, but it's like trying to stop the waves of the ocean from breaking. The demand is just too great. There are too many men in the world who enjoy forcing children into sexual slavery.

Once I went to Phnom Penh, the capital of Cambodia, on a fact-finding mission for my foundation. There is a promenade where tourists go, and there you can find dozens of perverts seducing young children. Many of the bars have second floors where beds are kept. There I saw men paying to sleep with eight-year-old girls or six-year-old boys, and my stomach turned. I see that this continues to happen and I say to myself: "What can I do? I'm working like crazy for this cause, and it's as if I haven't done a thing."

It infuriates me to no end. Rage blinds me when I see a man pay $300 to have sex with an eight-year-old girl. It's something I just can't comprehend and I simply cannot accept. Any man who is capable of doing this is a criminal and should be buried alive to be consumed by the worms. And why does it make me so angry? Not because I have lived through it, but simply because it is inhuman, and I've witnessed this inhumanity with my own eyes. I've also seen the degradation of these children caught on camera; I have seen a video of five-year-old girls, terror in their eyes, being asked, "Do you do pum pum? Or ñum ñum?"

Horrified, they respond, "Ñum ñum, yes. No pum pum."

Ñum ñum refers to oral sex, and pum pum is everything else. On the video you can hear the criminal, who is showing the little girls as if they are merchandise. He says, "Here are the most expensive ones . . . the virgins." And when he opens the door, you see five girls, holding hands and trembling. Then a grotesque man appears licking his lips, and says, "Maybe that one, the third one. . . ."

The girls generally come from very poor families. One day a trafficker shows up at their home and tells the parents that if they give their girls up, $1,000 will be sent to them monthly. How can they possibly say no? A thousand dollars is the equivalent of five years of work. The parents see it as an opportunity to buy food and medicine, and tell their daughter that it is time to go to work.

And that's how the whole thing starts.

There are the traffickers who come with stories about being from a modeling agency. And this, of course, excites the girls and their mothers. What little girl hasn't dreamed of one day becoming a model? So they tell them that there is a European agency in the capital that's looking for girls who have eyes and hair just like hers, and that she will be featured on television and in fashion shows. Both the mothers and daughters eagerly accept. But the moment the girls are taken from their homes they are thrown into a brothel.

Every time I think I've heard it all, that there couldn't possibly be a more horrible story than the one I just heard, an even worse one appears. I attend conferences all over the world—in New York, Vienna, wherever the issue of human trafficking exists—and always find out about new cases that have been brought to light. And the most startling thing about it is realizing that I really know nothing about human malice. I have always wanted to believe that human beings are naturally good, but when I hear these stories I realize this is not the case: Just like there are individuals in the world who are incredibly good and generous, there are also people who are disgustingly evil. So harrowing are the atrocities that the moment always comes when I feel I should just give up and go home because no matter what I do, human trafficking is a tough battle. It's a massive and powerful monster.

It doesn't matter how many laws and regulations are in place to control human trafficking; there are too many countries in which laws are simply not obeyed. In other countries, the laws are outdated. For example, there are some very powerful countries in Latin America where prostitution is tolerated, and the constitution says that a boy becomes a man at eighteen, while a girl becomes an adult at twelve. Therefore, if you see a twelve-year-old girl on the side of the road selling her body, well, technically—and according to that country's law—she is considered to be an adult and has every right to be a prostitute. Is it immoral? I think anyone would agree that it is. However, is it illegal? No. And therein lies the tragedy.

That really frustrates me. I have to ask myself, when the very governments of certain countries are allowing this to happen, if they don't realize they are exploiting their own girls, their own citizens, then what is it that I am actually doing? Am I trying to abolish slavery in the twenty-first century?

But deep down I know it does not matter how hard it is or how impossible it may seem; I have to continue with my struggle. It is one of those tests in life we must all face. The most important things are never easy to accomplish, and the more important the cause, the more we have to struggle for it. Climbing to the top of a mountain doesn't happen in one jump.

One of the things that helped me to forge ahead was meeting a Scottish activist when I was in Cambodia. I told him that sometimes I want to abandon the cause because the reality of the struggle consistently brings me so much disappointment. It seems that it doesn't matter what I do or with whom I speak, because each day I hear about more young prostitutes or more children who are victims of rape. It's as if I take one step forward and twenty steps backward.

He listened to me attentively and then said something I will never forget: "Focus on the people you have helped. Each life that you save is nothing more and nothing less than a life. It is one less life that is enslaved. Don't focus on what you have not been able to accomplish, or on what is yet to be done. Focus on what you *have* been able to accomplish. You rescued three girls off the street. And tomorrow you may have the opportunity to save another one. That's something to celebrate."

He's right. To continue with this fight, like in any battle, it is crucial to focus on what has been accomplished, and the results yielded. To not give in to disappointment about the goals that must still be reached. Each individual life saved is a victory in this never-ending battle.

There's a story I love that perfectly illustrates the point this Scottish activist was trying to make. There was once a man who was walking along the seashore, and he came upon a place where there were thousands of fish thrown on the sand, suffocating without water. The man began to toss the fish into the sea. Another man who was strolling by saw this and asked: "What are you doing? You know you won't be able to save them all."

"No, I won't be able to save them all," said the first man. And as he hurled one of the fish into the water, he said: "But this one, I can save."

The moral of the story is obvious: Every step taken is important. Every effort makes a difference, no matter how small it might be.

For me this means dedicating even more time to my work as a spokesperson, helping to raise awareness about what is happening. On a personal level, I think I would rather be in the streets fighting in the trenches and saving children every single day. But I know I give more strength to the movement, to the cause, and to the activism if I put on a suit and tie and speak directly to the United States Congress about the horrors that go on. This is why I must speak with the lobbyists, with congressmen, and with all the influential people who can in some way contribute to this cause I have dedicated myself to, because laws must be created and then strictly upheld.

Sometimes it seems very difficult to me, because I didn't get into philanthropy to walk around in a suit and tie talking to others wearing a suit and tie. I got into philanthropy because my first contact was directly with those children. It was through this contact with them that I understood the urgency of the situation; seeing the smile of happiness on the face of a child who has been through such horrors is one of life's most beautiful gifts. But part of what I have learned along the way is that everyone has to help with the tools that have been given to him. So although I could easily spend my days walking through the streets of Calcutta looking for girls to rescue, the fact of my being a person in the public eye creates a whole other dimension of work I can do to help, which isn't something everyone is able to do.

MAKING NOISE

GENERALLY SPEAKING, I have always tried to live my life as low-key as possible; when I am offstage, I don't like to be the center of attention. In fact, when I started the foundation, I wanted to do it anonymously, because I was doing it from a personal desire to help children, not to show the world what I do in order to look good. Many people encouraged me to announce what I was doing, but the last thing I wanted was for people to think I was doing any of it to get attention or publicity. What mattered to me was helping the children in the best way possible, not for people to find out that "Ricky Martin does this" or "Ricky Martin does that." But some of the human trafficking activists I worked with a few years ago made me see I was wrong.

"What do you mean, you don't want people to know?" they said. "That's nonsense! We need your voice. We have spent years and years doing this, and most people ignore us. But if someone like you, an artist who is well known and respected by the public, starts to scream our message out to the world, don't you think there will be a difference? People will pay attention to you. Maybe they won't do what you say, but at least they will pay attention, and that alone is progress."

The fact that as an artist I can have the power to convince and create some type of awareness is amazing. Desmond Child once said to me, "Ricky, don't be ashamed of having that power. Use it! Not everyone has it. Everyone comes to the world with a mission, and that's why Mahatma Gandhi was and continues to be Mahatma Gandhi, Martin Luther King, Jr., was Martin Luther King, Jr., and the Dalai Lama is the Dalai Lama. I am not saying that you have to be like them, but man, when you talk, people listen."

People who do it to achieve media attention should not bother doing it at all. They should do it only if it comes directly from their heart. However, I cannot blame the person who doesn't do it. Perhaps some of my colleagues have not lent their voices to any cause because they have not yet found the one that moves and motivates them. It might be that until now they have not found themselves face-to-face with the problem that will force them to stand up and say, "Enough already!" I worked like crazy for thirteen years before having this awakening. And although it is tempting to think about everything I could have done if I had started earlier, the truth is that I wouldn't have been able to do it. Remember: In life, everything arrives in its moment, and not before or after. I met those girls at the exact moment I needed to meet them, because that was when I was ready to give more. I worked hard ever since I was a little boy toward something I adored, music. And I did it because I wanted to do it, not because I was forced to. My childhood was amazing and unique. If I chose this cause it is because it appeared on my path and touched me deeply. It moved me. And I feel that if I see something I don't agree with, and don't do anything about it, then I am somehow allowing it to happen; it's like I am an accomplice. If we, who are all here together on this earth, don't take care of one another, then who else will? It is our duty. All of us have some responsibility on the spiritual path. It could be fighting against human trafficking; helping the elderly; assisting the helpless; fighting for the rights of the LGBT community (Lesbian, Gay, Bisexual, Transgender); or feeding the hungry—but we all have the obligation to stand up for what we believe in and help the less fortunate and take care of the neediest.

So we started to make some noise. I began to do more and more because I wanted to create a consciousness: I wanted the whole world to listen to what I have to say, and to believe that together we can fight against this epidemic. And it seemed that making noise worked, because after a very short time, many well-known and credible organizations took interest in forming alliances with the Ricky Martin Foundation. These alliances were very important, because I knew there wasn't a whole lot I could do on my own. In the world of nonprofits, alliances are crucial. Even though I may have a very clear idea of what I want to do, it doesn't mean I necessarily know how to do it. It's one thing to say, "I want to help the girls," and it's something entirely different to go out into the field and help them. That's why I had to find other organizations that had experience working for the causes that most mattered to me. From that point on, we began to work with such institutions as the Inter-American Development Bank, UNICEF, Save the Children, ATEST (Alliance to End Slavery and Trafficking), Johns Hopkins University, the International Organization for Migration, the University of Puerto Rico, the Florida Coalition Against Human Trafficking, and even Microsoft.

One of the programs we developed with Microsoft was aimed at a specific problem. Unfortunately, one of the easiest ways to traffic children is through the Internet. Traffickers make their way into chat forums and the children begin chatting with them and making friends, of course without knowing they are chatting with an adult. And while the parents think their kids are chatting with their friends, they are really talking with a trafficker right from the living room of their own home. It's completely terrifying. To raise awareness about this problem, we joined forces with Microsoft to create a program called *Navega Protegido* (Navigate Safely), with the purpose of protecting children in cyberspace. *Navega Protegido* is a campaign that educates parents and teachers alike, regarding all the risks that exist for a child when they are surfing the Web.

Even though we cannot completely prevent this type of thing from happening, at least we can raise awareness. We placed ads in public transportation systems that said: "Do you know who is chatting with your daughter?" And in airports, where kidnapped children are boarded on planes to other countries, we placed ads that say: "Do you know where you are traveling to? Did you meet this person on the Internet?"

After that, we launched a project called *Llama y Vive* (Call and Live), a toll-free hotline where victims of human trafficking can call for help. We conducted media campaigns to promote the phone numbers and received an amazing response. One day, a woman arrived at one of the radio stations on which the numbers had been advertised, and said: "Hi, I heard about your *Llama y Vive* campaign, and I don't have a phone. But I am a victim." Of course, the radio station personnel called the authorities right away, who in turn got in touch with us to help this woman with her rehabilitation. And just like that, we saved one more. Every single life matters.

The efforts of the Ricky Martin Foundation continue to expand, and we're always looking for new ways to fight human trafficking. At the beginning of 2010, in collaboration with the financial corporation Doral, we launched a new community program to mobilize social consciousness. I am convinced that this is a problem we can solve. No matter how massive it is, no matter how rampant it may be in countries all over the world, I know we have been able to create more of a consciousness; and maybe if people see the dangers faced by the world's children with their own eyes, we can make a difference.

NATURAL DISASTERS

ONE OF THE things very few people know about human trafficking is that traffickers often take advantage of extreme situations, such as earthquakes, floods, or wars, to abduct the children who are most vulnerable. Some of the most intense experiences I've lived through since I began fighting human trafficking have been when I have visited places affected by natural disasters, such as the tsunami of 2004 and the 2010 earthquake in Haiti. I will never in my life be able to erase those images from my mind, and the truth is that I don't want to: I don't want to forget about all the destruction, the pain, and the desolation I saw because I don't want to forget that each day I must continue fighting for my cause.

The tsunami unfurled at 9:33 a.m. on December 26, 2004, on the beaches of Patong, Thailand. According to witnesses, the first wave measured some thirty feet in height. It destroyed everything in its path. It overturned cars, crumbled buildings, knocked trees over, crushing the debris with its turbulent waters. The waves caused massive damage and thousands of deaths in Indonesia, Thailand, Sri Lanka, India, Somalia, and the Maldives. In its wake, it left a death toll of more than 287,000, and more than 50,000 missing people. A third of the dead were children.

Even though the news traveled through all the media, I didn't find out until several days later. I was on a private island in Puerto Rico celebrating my birthday with a group of friends. Even though the island had every form of communication, I wanted to remain disconnected, and a whole week went by without my looking at my cell phone once. I didn't know what was going on in Puerto Rico, never mind on the other side of the world. I was just having a good time, swimming in the ocean, relaxing on the sand, singing and playing music.

So it was not until January 3 or 4, when I returned to San Juan, that I found out about the tsunami. My first reaction was of complete anguish. I thought that if the tsunami had been in the Atlantic instead of on the other side of the world, I would have probably disappeared off the face of the earth, because I was on such a flat island that there was nowhere to run. I think that because I had just come back from so many days relaxing by the ocean, it hit me even harder to think that on the other side of the planet the ocean had actually turned into a monster.

I was completely and utterly jolted. I watched the chaos on television, all the devastation, heard the reports of the thousands of dead and still missing, and the children who were lost and in search of their parents, who by this point could be God only knows where. And suddenly I realized this was a perfect scenario for traffickers: There were thousands of traumatized kids, orphans, lost and helpless, who were willing to take help from anyone who was willing to give it. Once this way of thinking crossed my mind, there was no way to erase it. I knew these children were at risk and I had to do something about it. And fast.

I called the executive director of the foundation and I said to him, "We have to go to Thailand right away."

"Okay," he said, "and what are we going to do there?"

"I don't know!" I replied. "I just know that we have to go and we have to make noise so that people will pay attention to what is happening."

I knew it was one of those moments when it would be critical to utilize my power of conviction. I was ready to stand on any rooftop of any building and scream out, "Heads up! Children might be trafficked right now. They might be getting abducted as we speak!"

And that is more or less what we did. We invited a Puerto Rican writer who had traveled with us a lot. Every time we would go on a mission to Jordan or Calcutta, she would join us to document everything that happened on the trips. As we got ready to depart, we received a call from a producer of the *Oprah Winfrey Show* to ask if we were going to do something. So we invited her to join us as well, and that's how we ended up accompanied by cameramen from one of the most-watched television shows in the world. It was hard to imagine a more perfect alliance. We had not yet arrived, but we knew we were definitely going to make some noise!

We departed on a plane from San Juan to New York, to then fly from New York to London, and onward from London to Bangkok. While we were on the flight from New York to London, with the press and cameras on the plane with us, we still had no itinerary. The trip came to be so suddenly that we didn't even have time to plan what we were going to do. The way things were going, we were going to land in Bangkok and have to tell everyone, "Please just wait here while we rent a car. . . ." I talk about it now and it makes me laugh, but at that moment our minds were racing because we had no detailed plan of what we were going to do, which isn't at all how I was used to working, and surely Oprah's team wasn't, either. But this was a mission that came directly from the heart, and in the midst of the chaos I constantly kept repeating, in the form of a mantra, "Everything will be okay. Everything will be okay."

While we were in New York, the executive director of the foundation had been on the phone with the Thai embassy in Washington, D.C., telling them that Ricky Martin was en route to their country and wanted to help in whatever way possible. I was taking the activists' advice to not be afraid to use my name for a cause I believed in.

We arrived at London's Heathrow Airport, and my executive director again contacted the Thai embassy in Washington, and learned that the ambassador was extremely happy that we wanted to help and offered his full support. Once again, the planets aligned so that everything would flow magically. Or maybe it's just that the power of the mind is amazing. In those hours of total stress, my mantra helped a lot—that, I don't doubt for a second.

By the time we arrived in Bangkok, everything was resolved. We were picked up at the airport and we had a meeting with the prime minister, where we were briefed on what had taken place, and how the situation was being handled. Then they took us to the areas that had been most affected by the tsunami.

It was incredible. The earthquake that caused the tsunami shook the streets on the island of Phuket at 7:58 a.m., local time, toppling over pedestrians and motorcycle riders and causing drivers to lose control of their cars. The magnitude of the earthquake, 9.1 on the Richter scale, is considered the third highest since the existence of the seismograph; it was so strong it made the entire planet tremble and move from its axis almost one degree. The principal epicenter was almost five hundred kilometers from Phuket, west of Sumatra, at the bottom of the ocean. (The largest magnitude that has ever been registered was during the Great Earthquake of Chile in 1960, also known as the Valdivia earthquake, which caused a tsunami that devastated Hilo, Hawaii, more than ten thousand kilometers from the epicenter.)

The first tremor lasted for more than eight minutes. When it was over, the worst was still to come. Approximately an hour and a half after the earthquake, the people who were on the beaches of Phuket noticed that the ocean began to quickly recede. Some went to investigate and to pick up some of the fish that were left stranded on dry land with the sudden retreat of the water. Those who were on Mai Khao beach on the north of the island were very lucky, because a ten-year-old British girl had studied tsunamis in a geography class in elementary school and recognized the signs of an imminent tsunami. She explained it to her parents and the family alerted everyone else on the beach, and all of them were able to escape. Not far from there, a Scottish teacher also recognized the signs of what was coming and was able to take a bus full of tourists and local residents to safety.

Unfortunately, the same thing did not occur in other areas. Many went out to investigate, or stayed in place calmly without even realizing what was happening. The first swell came minutes later, and the impact hurled boats and cars into the air, destroyed homes, and ripped trees out of the ground.

The second wave came thirty minutes later, and thirty minutes after that came the strongest one of all, which was estimated at almost one hundred feet tall. That one turned the streets into a violent and muddled river, full of debris that flooded up to the second floor of many buildings and damaged miles of beach.

All throughout the Indian Ocean there were more tsunamis of similar magnitude, crashing against the coasts of Bangladesh, Indonesia, Sri Lanka, and, seven hours after the initial earthquake, in Somalia. The tsunami was the most lethal in history and left an entire region so devastated that it is still struggling to fully recover today.

When I arrived in Thailand, some ten days after the earthquake happened, they took me to the Pang Na region and told me there were other areas where the damage was five times worse than what I was seeing. It's really hard for me to imagine that, because where I was standing the situation looked very grim. The school was transformed into a hospital, someone's home became a school, and the Buddhist temple was now a morgue. So the temple, that place where one normally goes to find some sort of spiritual life, was now populated by physical death. Stop and think about that for a moment.

But in the midst of so much devastation, there was also hope. Many children had been orphaned, but I felt that I could still do something for them. What happens in times like this, as I explained before, is that the traffickers take advantage of the situation during natural disasters. They take advantage of the hopelessness of the situation and literally go fishing in the streets. They know there will be many lost children, without families to protect them and completely scared. When they come upon a child who is crying for his mother, they know that this child will believe anyone who says, "I know where your parents are. Come with me."

And that's how they are taken. And that's exactly why I wanted to go there. Wherever there is a natural disaster, where there is chaos, it offers the opportunity that a trafficker seeks to exploit, taking advantage of the most vulnerable and stealing their most basic human rights.

At a hospital where orphans were being lodged, I met the youngest survivor of the tsunami, who had been dubbed Baby Wave. Baby Wave appeared in the center of the city floating on a mattress when he was only days old. Someone had stuck a note to his clothes that said: "I found this boy in the beach area, but I have no food to give him. I have nothing for him. Please, take care of him."

It was a miracle in the midst of all the destruction, so the nurses were protecting him as if he was a little jewel. But they had to hide him in an office and monitor him day and night, because when the press got wind of the fact that the youngest survivor of the tsunami had been found, people came from all over claiming to be his parents or perhaps an uncle. But when the nurses said they would be happy to administer a DNA test, they would all disappear.

There were people who even pretended to be doctors, saying they had to take him to another hospital for this or that exam. It was all a lie. They were all traffickers who wanted to take him and sell him or God knows what. The love the nurses showed in their protection of Baby Wave was inspiring, and holding him in my arms was another moment in my life I will always remember. He represented hope.

In the midst of so much death and suffering, I also saw some very beautiful things. I met, for example, the woman who transformed her house into a school because she felt it important that the surviving children not be left without one. It was a very modest house, with a mud floor, located in a small Thai fishing town. Every morning sixty kids would show up, and she would sit them in a small area inside the house, where she set up a chalkboard so they could read and write. They were of all ages, up to nine or ten years old. They had little chairs and used some wooden boards as tables. Maybe for us that's not much, but the truth is that they weren't missing a thing. They had food and water, a calm and clean house to learn in, and someone to look after them.

The woman who opened her home in this way was very intelligent because she knew it was not only about the children continuing on with their studies; she knew what they really needed was to stay busy and occupied. It was important that they kept their minds active so that they wouldn't have time to think about the great tragedy they were living through. The fact that they could stay with her all day kept them safe, because if those kids had not been at school or another place where they could be protected, the traffickers could have come to take them.

That woman saw these children's needs and did whatever she could to help. And the one who dedicated herself to those sixty children during that gruesome tragedy made a monumental difference in their lives.

After spending a few days visiting the various damaged areas, I returned to Puerto Rico and held a fund-raiser. It was a breakfast in San Juan, where I met business leaders and other distinguished individuals from the island. At the breakfast I gave a testimony of all that I had seen in Thailand. I spoke to them about the pain I felt upon seeing so much destruction and the anger I felt over what was happening, and I invited them to join me in helping these damaged areas. Just like the Swiss, the Norwegians, the Finnish, the Russians, the Chinese, and the Indians were all working to lend a hand. I needed us in Puerto Rico to also do something. *Anything.*

And that's how it went. Those people and more contributed so that we would be able to build homes for some of the victims of the most damaged areas in Thailand. But since I don't have the knowledge or experience for this type of project, we allied ourselves with Habitat for Humanity, a global nonprofit organization dedicated to building safe and decent homes for people in need in over ninety countries around the world. I spoke with the prime minister of Thailand, and he was very amiable and helped me to find land where these homes could be built. The majority of the funds that were raised for the construction came through various collaborative efforts of my foundation, and then we matched the amount donated. Together with the connections and expertise provided by Habitat for Humanity, and all the local and international volunteers who donated their time in support of our joint efforts, as well as the local people who donated additional construction materials for the homes, we were able to build 224 homes in total.

It gave me tremendous satisfaction. We all mixed cement and lent a hand. I placed the cement against the bricks and then cut the bricks. The truth is that I had never done construction work before, but there were many people there volunteering who had never laid a brick, either. And we all had a great time. At the time, I didn't get to see any of the houses fully completed, but I was able to finish a wall that will hopefully remain part of that family's home forever.

But that wasn't the end of the story. After spending a few days in Thailand I did the other part of my duty: I returned to the United States to appear on the *Oprah Winfrey Show*, to talk to the world about what was going on. We ran the video of me visiting one of the most damaged areas, and we showed the people not only what we had done but also everything that was still (and still is) left to do.

It is likely that there are people who think I did what I did for publicity. If that is the case, let them all think what they like. Maybe a few years back I might have felt the need to justify my actions. But now I know the only thing that really matters is what I think. My only objective was to get people to understand the need for help in these damaged areas, and to show them everything that can be done to help. There are so many ways of helping, and on so many different levels, that I believe everyone should find a way to do it, be it with money, time, or anything else. In any case, I felt so proud of what we had done. Especially when a few months later I had the privilege of going back to Thailand to hand the keys to the family that would move into the home we had begun building during my previous trip, and to meet additional families that would move into some of the other homes we sponsored. That was another day I will always remember. In total, more than one thousand people in two tsunami-affected areas ended up permanently benefiting from the work we had done.

I could see the expressions of joy in those families when they walked into their new homes for the first time, and I thanked the cosmos for giving me the chance to help. I also gave thanks for having been able to see firsthand how these families were rebuilding their lives with love, which united them and gave them the strength to face and overcome anything.

Something similar happened at the beginning of 2010 when a brutal earthquake shook all of Haiti. Upon seeing the first images on television, and being intensely moved by the proximity of Haiti and Puerto Rico, I felt that I had to go there as soon as possible to see how I could help. But just like with the tsunami in Thailand, a lot of people tried to talk me out of it, saying, "That's total chaos there, Ricky. What are you going to do over there?" But like with the tsunami, I felt deep in my soul that it was something I had to do. I had to go there and walk the streets and live what our Haitian brothers and sisters were living, to really know what I could do to help. Just being there I could feel, resonate, and understand what was going on in order to lend a hand.

And the truth is that I could never have imagined what I would find upon arriving in Port-au-Prince. It was absolute chaos, but a chaos unlike anything I had ever seen before, even in Thailand. The structures were all collapsed—there were areas were there was literally not one single building left standing—and the streets were littered with corpses and remains of the dead wherever you looked. On top of that, there was zero organization. While in Thailand there was some semblance of order via the government and the local entities that still stood, in Haiti there was nothing. There was no government structure in charge and not even community leaders, because the majority had perished. Being in Haiti was like living in some kind of living hell; I have never seen anything like it. The devastation was such that even the organizations that specialized in the recovery and aftermath of natural disasters, professionals on the subject, were completely lost and didn't know where to begin.

Like in Thailand, after visiting the most damaged area, we decided that the best way to help would be by building homes, the idea being once again that if children have homes to come back to, they will stay off the streets, where they are most vulnerable to the traffickers. With all of our foundation projects, we always try to think in terms of the big picture. It's not about finding a solution just for today and tomorrow alone. We want to find ways of helping that are permanent and serve to prevent more tragedies or dangerous situations in the future.

So we again joined forces with Habitat for Humanity, and together we are implementing both short-term and long-term housing solutions for children and families in Haiti. We have already provided emergency temporary shelter and housing solutions to hundreds affected by the quake, and soon we will begin construction on permanent homes. Once again, our alliance is providing safety and shelter for children whose lives could otherwise be in danger as a result of this natural disaster, and by doing so we are providing hope for their futures. I can't wait to meet the Haitian families and hand them the keys to their permanent homes, which will be built with love, just as the homes in Thailand were. In the meantime, with the collaboration of many colleagues from the entertainment world, I recorded a series of public service announcements (in English and Spanish) urging the world to help Haiti. Slowly but surely we are making a difference, as tiny as it may seem in the sea of problems that Haiti faces today. Once again, here, like with so many different aspects of my life, I have learned that I have to focus on what I have done, as opposed to what is left to do. Otherwise, it would be too overwhelming.

SEVEN

FATHERHOOD

SOONER OR LATER WE ALL REACH A POINT WHEN WE aspire to do more with our lives. We begin to realize that it is no longer enough to simply exist in the world, and we feel the need to transcend who we are to become something greater. For me, that aspiration manifested itself in my desire to be a father.

Even though my work battling human trafficking in some way did fulfill my desire to do something I felt was important, I cannot say that it was enough to completely fill my soul. I had arrived at a point in my life where I simply wanted more: a family of my own. For me, having a child means you are ready to give yourself entirely, and that's exactly how I was feeling. I no longer wanted to wait for the right moment or the perfect partner to do it: I was ready to be a father, and once I understood this, I did what I had to do to turn my dream into a reality.

MAKING THE LEAP

IN TRUTH, IT started with Baby Wave, because when I met him the first thing I thought was that I wanted to adopt him.

At the time, I was told that single fathers are not allowed to adopt in Thailand, so it was not even an option. However, that little one's tenderness, and his strength and determination to live, awoke something very profound within me.

The second catalyst came when a friend of mine became pregnant. It was wonderful because this friend also happened to be my physical therapist, so I was around her during her entire pregnancy. She accompanied me on the Black and White Tour in 2007, so each day I could see how her belly was growing, and the fact that I was so close to her during those nine months helped me to experience the miracle of life. She eventually got to a point where she could no longer travel and had to stay home, but when her precious little daughter was born, I felt something click inside. Like so many other times, my moment had arrived. And that is how my search began.

Meeting that tiny baby in the chaos of the tsunami and then seeing my friend's utter happiness when she gave birth made a huge impression on me. Both events triggered a deep peace and sense of joy so pure that I somehow wanted to bring that feeling into my own life. I felt that my moment to be a father had come. At last, the only thing that mattered was that I was ready to be a father, and as far as that feeling went, no one was going to tell me otherwise: not my family, my friends, nor my lovers. This is something I felt I needed, something I desperately wanted to do, and so I set out to find the best possible way to do it.

In hindsight, I realize my path had been leading up to this moment and had given me all of the tools I would need to make this decision. I had not only learned to accept and love myself; I had at last found the role of my life—working for the cause against human trafficking—and now I felt ready to unconditionally love someone else. Though I suppose no one is ever really ready to become a parent—in large part because it isn't until one is a parent that one can truly understand what it means—in that moment I felt I had developed the spiritual tools necessary to take this very critical step.

The time I spent in India helped me a lot. There I learned to listen to my silence, and therefore get to know myself, but I also learned a lot about life. I needed some distance from my career to learn the simple things about life and to be able to share my time here with others. Because I had spent so much time running around trying to be number one, I did not have time to grow up and mature at my own pace. I had to learn how to cry, to walk through the streets and see other people; I had to take control of my own life.

In India I learned how to focus on gratitude. I think that most of us—myself included—go through life focusing on the negative. We often think we're doing this to be realistic, or simply because we are identifying the negative things we are trying to eliminate in our lives. And although I don't think we are wrong when we pay attention to that which hurts and bothers us—if we are really doing it for the sake of making things better—I believe it's also important to dedicate time to focus on the good things, so we can repeat them and increase them in our lives.

Today, when I feel bad, or when the day seems to weigh me down, or when I feel there is a cloud chasing me around everywhere I go, I make a list of ten things I am grateful for.

Just ten. At first, when I would try to do this, I couldn't get past three. I would think: "I'm alive. I'm healthy. There is food on my table . . . ," and that's as far as I would get. It would take me a long time to be able to expand that list.

But when I really stop to think, I realize there are so many more extraordinary things to be grateful for. I can walk. I can see. I can feel. I have friends. I have a family that loves me. I have a home. I have two beautiful sons. And by the time I get to number eight on the list, I am already smiling. And that's how I focus on the positive, which means adding instead of taking away.

I always knew I was destined to be a father. It wasn't like at age twenty-five I said, "When I am thirty-six I'll do it." I simply felt that my moment had arrived, and faced it when I knew I was ready. I know there are many people who are afraid to be parents, and I can honestly say it never worried me at all. I had the extraordinary example of my father. When he married his second wife, she said to me, "I fell in love with him because of how he treated you. I saw the dynamic between the two of you and I said to myself, 'This is the type of father that I want for my children.'" And it's true. We have always had an incredible relationship, full of open communication and understanding, and this is the type of relationship I want to have with my own children.

Besides, until the moment when I joined Menudo I felt like the best brother, because I taught my youngest brothers, my father's sons, how to ride a bike, tie their shoes, and so many other basic childhood things. Later, when I joined Menudo, it hurt me to think I had abandoned my younger siblings, and I often felt that the eldest of them would look at me with an expression that seemed to say, "Where were you when I needed you?"

But I later understood that I had to absolve myself of this melancholic attitude, and of the guilt I always carried for having left, because I finally understood that life took me down a certain path that distanced me from him, and that's simply how it was. It was no one's fault. It was a lesson for both of us and it never took away from the fact that I adore him, along with the rest of my brothers. The proof is that today we are all very close, we see each other at every opportunity, and we love each other so much. And it is because of this very special relationship I have with them and with my parents that I always felt I wanted to be a father.

The more I considered the pros and cons of the various alternatives that exist to have children, the one that sounded best was surrogate motherhood. Now, I'd like to clarify that this was the best option for *me*. I'm not out to convince the rest of the world about surrogacy, nor will I stand on a mountaintop and scream that surrogacy is the most amazing thing that has ever happened. I am aware that this may not be the best option for everyone, but it was for me. I already knew I didn't want to start a family with a woman, and since I also didn't want to wait to find the love of my life in order to have children, I decided this was the way to go.

When I told my mother what I was going to do, she looked at me and said, "Wait a moment, Kiki. Sit down for a second so we can talk. What you are telling me sounds like some kind of film from the future."

"No, Mami. This isn't the future," I answered. "This is the present."

And I explained to her how everything works. When I finished, the only thing she said to me was, "My son, you have to have your head screwed on the right way to make this kind of decision. Congratulations."

Some people may not be fully aware of what surrogacy is and therefore find it strange, or even might think it is something negative. But the truth is that it's an excellent alternative that we have today, thanks to all the medical advances that science has been able to accomplish. To think that previously, when a couple was not able to conceive a child, they would have to resign themselves to that fact without many options. Today, a couple that cannot have children—or has difficulty doing so—has all kinds of options available to them.

The surrogacy process takes time. It's not just the nine months of pregnancy. It starts a lot earlier. I wanted to do it through an agency that specializes in this, and, obviously, I wanted a lawyer with expertise in the field who could guide me throughout the whole process. And that's how I did it.

Surrogacy is becoming more and more common each day. Even though there are no hard statistics, it is estimated that since 1976 there have been approximately twenty-eight thousand children born through a surrogate, and every day there are more single parents who opt to have children this way. More than ever, men are becoming more conscious of the meaning of fatherhood and feel the need to have children whether they have a partner (be it a man or a woman) or not.

The first step in my own surrogacy process after finding the agency and then the attorney I wanted to work with was to select a donor for my eggs. I spent an entire week examining the bios of women who were offering their eggs. Even though I knew I wanted to find someone who embodied qualities that would complement my own, it was still very hard to choose the right person. Perhaps if I had fallen in love with someone it wouldn't have been so difficult; we would simply be in love and have babies. But this was another story, and to choose a person based on their bio didn't turn out to be as easy as I had thought it would be.

Once I chose the egg donor, the next step was to find the woman who would lend her belly to carry the baby. My lawyers advised that it would be best to do it anonymously. They explained that the mothers who carry babies are completely used to that, and some of them even prefer it because it makes it seem as if they are pregnant with their own child and they can go about their lives perfectly normally. In fact, most cases of surrogate motherhood are handled privately and with no contact, as if it was a closed adoption. There are open adoptions in which all parties agree to remain in contact and are known to each other, but there are also closed adoptions, where women who are giving their babies up for adoption don't want to have any contact at all with the baby or with the parents who are going to raise him or her. And often, the adoptive parents also don't want to have any kind of connection with the biological mother. This is a similar thing. The mothers who donate their eggs or carry the babies understand and accept the fact that the mother or father who will raise the child has chosen not to have any ties to those who have helped bring the child into the world.

Open surrogacy also exists, in which the surrogate mother can be in contact with the family, and eventually with the child. It all depends on what's best in each individual case. In my case, I felt it would be best to have a closed surrogacy.

I stayed in touch with the surrogate mother throughout her entire pregnancy. But we did it anonymously. I was also in touch with her doctors regularly. Even though I was not by her side physically, I was with her throughout the entire pregnancy and I made sure she received the best care possible.

If my sons want to know about their egg donor when they are older, I will be able to show them photographs of her. They have a right to know who she is; she is part of their genetic history. But she asked that we not have any contact. She says she really didn't have much to do with this, and that she doesn't necessarily have the desire to have children. She said she did it for the simple fact of being able to help others to form a family, and that is enough of a blessing.

Meanwhile, the woman who carried the boys has no genetic connection to them. She simply lent her belly. I am very grateful for what she did, and if I do it again in the future, I would love for it to be she who carries my children again. She had already been through the process previously, and she came well recommended by the agency. When I interviewed her, I asked her why she was doing it, and she responded: "I am a very spiritual woman, and I have never felt as close to God as when I am able to give the gift of life to someone who cannot do it on their own."

I loved her response. I felt that we were aligned in our beliefs and her words inspired my great respect for her. For me it was an honor that a woman like her would take care of my children for nine months, and I am eternally grateful to her for the calm and healthy environment she provided for them.

I started this whole process when I was on the Black and White Tour. It was around August of 2007 when I first typed the word "surrogacy" into a search engine and began to learn everything I could about the subject. Shortly thereafter, I began the process of selecting an egg donor and the woman who would lend her belly, along with all the medical tests and legal documents that are required. The tour ended in November, and approximately one month later I found out that the surrogate mother was pregnant. That year I celebrated New Year's by giving thanks for the miraculous gift that awaited me.

Typically in surrogacy, two embryos are implanted to increase the possibility of success, and to avoid the possibility of having to go through the whole process multiple times. But even though I always knew there were two embryos, I figured I was only going to have one child. Of course, as if it wasn't enough to become a father, life had yet another surprise for me, and this one came about two weeks into the pregnancy when they told me I was going to have twins!

A close friend who knows me well and who has worked with me for over twenty years said, "Man, can't you do anything normal in your life? You always have to do things outrageously. . . . It seems that for you this is the only way!"

I can't begin to describe my joy when I found out there was going to be two of them. . . . It was incredibly emotional. I started to prepare myself to be the single father of two children, and I read everything I could find. The only problem was that I was short one name, and this seemed like a major problem to me, because it had been hard enough to come up with the first one! I'd searched through so many cultures: I looked at India, Brazil, Egypt. . . . I even looked at the names of some of the Taino Indians, the indigenous natives of the island of Puerto Rico. I'd finally decided he would be called Matteo, a Jewish name that means "gift from God."

But now I needed to find another, and quickly, because until that point we were referring to the baby as "Baby B" (as they labeled them on the sonograms). Still, it was not as difficult as choosing the first one. I closed my eyes and visualized a brave and fearless child. For this reason, I called him Valentino, because he is like a warrior: Valentino the valiant one.

Time has never moved more slowly in my head than during those next six months. They seemed eternal. Naturally, when a woman is pregnant with twins there is always a greater risk for complications, which of course concerned me, and I was always in close touch with the woman carrying the children, making sure that everything was running smoothly.

But in the midst of it all, what I felt in the deepest part of my soul can only be described as unadulterated bliss. Absolute happiness. I imagine that anyone who has children will wholeheartedly agree it's like spending nine months waiting for the most incredible gift of all. All I wanted to do was stand on my rooftop and scream the great news out to the world. But I had to be very cautious, because I didn't want anything to affect the woman who was carrying my children. I wanted her to be calm and maintain her inner peace so that her pregnancy would proceed without complications. If for whatever reason the media found out what was going on, they might have discovered who she was and then barraged her with questions and intruded on her everyday life. Besides not wanting people to bother her because I didn't want anything to affect her or my children, I felt terribly responsible for imposing so much pressure and invading someone else's privacy. It has been my choice to lead a public life, and for that I accept the consequences; but I would never want to impose that on someone else.

So to ensure that the secret would be kept from the rest of the world, with the exception of my parents, I only told three people. It's not that I didn't trust the rest of my friends, but I was nervous that it might mistakenly slip from someone's lips out of sheer excitement, which would have been a disaster. There were even some friends—and this is when you realize who your true friends really are— who asked me not to talk to them about it, because if the news were to somehow get out to the press, they didn't want to find themselves on the list of people who might be responsible. . . . They were with me at all times making sure I was okay, but they didn't want to know more than what was necessary. And I will always be grateful for that loyalty and affection.

Like a good first-time father, while I waited for the boys to be born I read every book there was to read: child development books, books about twins, books about the first weeks of life. In fact, there are remarkably few books available about being a single father (and those that are available primarily focus on what to do after divorce), and I wanted to be fully informed on the subject by the time they were born. So I spent all of my time reading, learning, preparing. My mind was like a sponge; I wanted to know anything and everything about how to be the best father possible. At the same time, I was fully aware that most of what it's really like to be a father can't be learned in any book, nor passed on from person to person. It's an instinct that only shows itself when you hold your baby in your arms, and learn to interpret his various cries, laughs, smiles, and motions. An instinct that you never know you have until you reach that moment.

I was at the hospital when they came into the world. My sons were born via a C-section, and immediately after they were born they were brought to my room, where the incubator/warmer was waiting for them. There was a nurse there who checked all their vitals: their pulses, temperatures, color, size, everything. She shook those poor little boys, and they would tremble as they cried. Even though I was so excited that I felt I might explode, I didn't cry. Not even a little bit. I was so elated that I wanted to scream, "Give them to me!" I wanted to say to the nurse the minute she came into the room, "I want to hold them right now!"

The next few weeks were almost a blur. Like almost all new parents, I was totally obsessed with my children. I didn't want to miss a moment of their existence. They were the most beautiful babies I have ever seen, and I stared at them constantly. I almost never put them down when they were awake. And I didn't sleep. In your more "typical" newborn household, there are usually two parents and one baby; shared responsibility; and a little time to rest. In my case, it was two babies and one parent, and rest wasn't an option. But I didn't care. Don't get me wrong. I was never alone during those days; I was always surrounded by the people I love most, and everyone was more than willing to help. But there are certain things I wanted to do on my own. (You know, little things like feeding, bathing, diapering, and putting the babies to sleep.) And because I do everything to the extreme, I wanted to do it for both of them at exactly the same time.

I have a close friend who is a doctor, and she reminded me that I had to keep them on a schedule or it would simply be impossible for everyone. But the one thing I forgot to do was to keep myself on the same schedule! As any new parent knows, there's a basic rule: When the baby sleeps, you sleep. Period. Whether it's for ten minutes or an hour, it may be the only sleep you get that day. But I refused; I was so enamored of them that when they slept, the only thing I wanted to do was just watch *them* sleep! It got to a point where my mother (who was with me from the day they were born) said to me, "Son, you are a zombie. You are talking to me and falling asleep in the middle of what you are saying. Please, please put your head on the pillow and get some rest. You are an incredible father, but please, let us help you." I listened to her and was asleep within seconds. But that's literally what it took for me to close my eyes and get some rest. I just didn't want to miss a single moment of my sons' lives. I still don't. But I learned an important lesson in those first few weeks: that I need to take care of myself so that I am able to take care of them.

I will never forget the moment that each of them looked into my eyes for the very first time. Those were the most precious moments in my entire life. The moments I hadn't even realized I had been waiting for. They were *OUR* moments.

It wasn't until a few weeks later that the tears finally came. I had sat down to watch some television while the boys were asleep, and a show came on that mentioned the birth of my sons—by then the news had leaked out to the press. The anchorwoman suddenly looked at the camera and said, "We are very happy for you, Ricky. You deserve all the best. Congratulations!" Then everything hit me at once. I think it finally clicked right then that these two little ones who were sleeping in their cribs were actually *my* sons! And I was their *father*! It was a beautiful thing. But a very intense feeling coursed through my entire being, a joy so profound I couldn't stop crying. My father came over and hugged me for a long time—it was incredibly overwhelming.

ALL KINDS OF FAMILIES

THERE ARE PEOPLE who say that this isn't fair, that in order to have balance, children need a mother and a father. And I say they are mistaken. How many millions of children grow up without a mother? Or moreover, how many of them grow up with a mother who does not love them? How many millions of kids grow up without a father? Or worse, knowing that their father exists, but doesn't get involved with their lives because he doesn't love them. According to the census bureau of the United States, the number of single parents who live with their children increased by 25 percent during the 1990s. When my sons ask me, I am going to say: "I wanted to have you so very badly that, with God's help, everything lined up so that you would come into my life."

I am also here to say that there are also many successful people who were raised without a mother or father. For example, the vice president of the United States, Joe Biden, was a single father who raised his sons after his wife and daughter were both killed in a car accident. The president of the United States, Barack Obama, was raised without a father. There are also the Olympic swimmer Michael Phelps, President Bill Clinton, Bill Cosby, Tom Cruise, Christina Aguilera, Julia Roberts, Demi Moore, Alicia Keys, Angelina Jolie . . . just to name a few. So, in this day and age, single-parent families may be more common than society would like to think. I also know plenty of people who grew up in a home with both a mother and father and have unfortunately turned out to be very lost, unhappy, and problematic human beings.

Besides, if you think that because I am a single father my boys are not surrounded by wonderful women, don't worry—they are. My mother, for example, plays a critical role in their lives, and informs me as a father. She is the firm hand that guides me, always teaching me about the endless hard work that goes into being a father. But above all else, she gives them all the love in the world, and then some. And many of my closest friends are incredible women who love my children like aunts. Ultimately that's what matters most: It is exactly the same thing if my sons receive love from a father, a mother, a grandparent, an aunt, an uncle, or a friend. The important thing is that they receive and continue to receive it for the rest of their lives.

My sons are growing up surrounded by people who adore them, and who want the best for them. I consider it a privilege. I want them to grow up with open minds, and to be surrounded by other children who have the same. They will have no problem being raised by a father who is both their father and mother. On the contrary: They will be proud of their family, because thanks to it, they will see the world without prejudices and without judging others. It is something I have noted in other children of single fathers who have done the same thing as me. They are kids who are on a very special level.

The day that Matteo and Valentino ask me why they don't have a mother, I will explain to them that every family is unique. There are families who have a father, a mother, and a baby. There are families who have a father, a mother, and two babies. There are families who have a father, a mother, and five babies. There are families who only have one mother with four or five babies. There are families who have two mothers and two babies. There are other families that consist of two people who love each other but don't have any babies. In this moment, my sons have a father who does the work of both a father and a mother with two babies, and that is what makes our family unique. And being unique is fabulous.

I am ready for the question because I know that when they are ready, they will ask it of me. The moment a child is able to process a question, it is because he is ready to receive information about the question and to understand the truth about the answer. If that answer has too much information for their mind, then they'll just ignore it and go on playing with their toys for another couple of months, until they are ready to ask the question again. Regardless of how many times they ask me and how many times I have to answer it, I will continue to explain it to them again and again until they comprehend it well.

I know I want to have more kids one day, because it has been so incredible to have them by my side, almost constantly. In the two years since they were born, I've never spent more than two nights away from them, and that was only once. Like most parents, I don't want to be away from them for even a moment, because every day brings something unique and new. I'm grateful to have the ability to organize my life to suit their needs, and I have the privilege of being present for all of their first milestones in life. I deeply treasure the time I spend with them, and I love watching everything they do and hearing all the things that have started coming out of their mouths. Even though they are twins, born on the same day, each one has his own personality and way of doing things. They are individuals, and yet they complement each other perfectly.

They have taught me lot. From them I have learned the meaning of unconditional love, and in my experience of love I can say there is nothing quite like this. It doesn't matter what I may be doing for them—be it feeding them, changing their diapers, or bathing them—what I always get back is a smile. It's truly all they have to give, and they give it to me, over and over again! When they flash that smile at me, I think, "The world could fall apart tomorrow, but it wouldn't matter to me. This is the greatest joy imaginable."

Most people give because they want to receive. It's like a transaction—if you love me, I'll love you, and if you give me a hug, I'll give it back to you. In couples' relationships, with colleagues, and with friends it is often like that, right? If you love me with two steps, I'll love you back with two steps. But this love is not like that. This is true love. With this love, there is nothing else to search for. And this type of love begins when one begins to love one's self. When we learn to accept and love ourselves just as we are, that's when we can start to give love without expecting anything in return. Then we will find that we receive so much more love than we could ever imagine. Because when others see that we are full of love and that we give without expectations, they are not afraid to fully open up.

I am concerned about the fact that my sons will have to

learn how to grow up in the public eye, and that there are people who are going to want to invade their personal lives for the simple fact that they are my sons. This makes me anxious, not only because it has already started but also because I wanted to avoid it completely. But unfortunately, or fortunately, this is the life they were given and this is the path they will have to take. And they'll simply have to handle it each in his own way.

What is certain is that I will not allow my children to grow up in a cage. Life should be lived fully, and in that regard, I want my boys to be healthy, to acquire their own character traits and personalities as they grow, through their individual life experiences. I don't want them to be afraid of anything; I want them to be transparent and free, and more than anything, I want them to travel and see the world.

When I was younger, I would often go alone to Europe for my birthday or New Year's. My mother would say to me, "Are you crazy? What's wrong with you? First of all, why do you have to go alone? And why do you have to go so far?"

And I would respond, "Mami, leave me alone. I'm fine here."

One night I had the urge to spend the night sitting under the Eiffel Tower, and so I did. I lay down in a park in front of the tower, and at midnight, I said to myself, "Happy New Year!" I did the same thing one time for my birthday. It was amazing to feel that I was doing exactly what I wanted to do, and that I was doing it for myself and no one else.

I want my children to have experiences of all kinds. I want them to be independent and to live the lives they've always dreamed of. I look forward to watching them each walk their own paths, on their terms, and I will support them every step of the way.

I am Puerto Rican and so are my sons. I want them to always be conscious of their roots, but more than anything, I want my children to see themselves as citizens of the world, because this is what is going to give them the global vision to be men in the twenty-first century.

I will always make every effort to give my children everything they need. But the important things in life are not material; they are experiences. I want them to have all kinds of memories, because that's what is going to allow them to live full lives.

And since I have firsthand experience in knowing how important it is to maintain that connection with our inner child, I will do everything I can to make sure they hold on to the innocence of their youth for many years. And throughout their lives I will do everything possible to protect their integrity as human beings. I am sure that nothing that I want for my children is any different from what other parents also want for their own kids.

To my children I will say, "I want you to be happy and to always know that my love is unconditional. And that means *without conditions*. I am here for you. *No matter what.*"

I want them to feel they can tell me anything and that I will listen to them and always tell them the truth. They cannot be afraid to tell me anything. They should know that whatever advice I give them will always come first from my own experience, and second from my love for them. Pure love. I'll say to them, "I am here for you. I can tell you what the consequences will be of certain actions or decisions, and I can tell you what I think will be the consequences of doing this or that thing, based on what I have seen and lived. I can show you statistics that indicate the various effects of different choices. But I cannot decide for you."

Ultimately, they will have to do what they want, to become who they would like to be. The truth is that it doesn't matter how much I may love them. They will always be who they are, and I will always be me. And I cannot change who they are or how they behave; I can simply guide them in what I feel is the most appropriate direction. So many books have been written about how to be a good parent, but every child is completely unique. Each little mind is its own universe, and each child is the owner of his actions.

It doesn't matter how much you love a person; the reality of life is that one cannot make decisions for someone else. Even if they do exactly what I say they should do, and even if they believe that they're doing it just because I told them to, it is they who have chosen to take that path and not go off on their own. And if they only do what I tell them, they will never be able to analyze a situation, evaluate the information that is given to them, weigh the options and look at the alternatives (and they will eventually resent me). They will have to learn how to do this on their own, because I will not always be there to give them my opinion or advice.

In fact, it could be that my concept of happiness will for them be the very same definition of pain. And who am I to tell other people what it is that will make them happy? They have to discover it for themselves.

For me, that's where the improvement of the world begins—in allowing people to be themselves, without judging them. Let me be who I am; let me live, exist, and behave how I need to according to my reality. I'll do the same for you. I won't get in your way. In this space of my own, I dream of my happiness. And if you don't like it, go on your own way, because I don't want you to be part of mine.

Ultimately, I want my children to accept themselves, to love themselves, and to accept everyone, even if someone does not accept them. I will do everything possible for my children to find their happiness, letting them know that inside we each have the ability to feel fulfilled, if we are open and attuned to the lessons that come along the way, and willing to uncover the treasure that lives within our very own beings.

They are of course too young to understand, but Matteo and Valentino have played an essential role in making me the strong and liberated person I am today. It is thanks to them that my desire to write this book came to be, and it is also thanks to them that I found the strength to choose to live life transparently and without any secrets. As my children grow up, I want them to feel perfectly free, and there will not be anything—not even their father's life—that will affect them. They have to feel completely proud of who they are and where they come from, and I never want them to feel the need to keep a secret from me or from anyone. They are my greatest treasure, and the ones who inspire me each day to be a better person, a better father, and a better human being.

EIGHT

MY MOMENT

WHEN I LOOK BACK, IT'S EASY TO SEE HOW ONE THING LED to the next, and how every moment of my life happened for a reason. But when I was in the middle of it all, looking ahead and trying to decipher the next step, it wasn't always so easy to see. Still, today I feel that it doesn't do any good to worry so much about what decision to make or which path to take, because ultimately life has its way of guiding me toward what I need when I need it the most. Not before, not after.

There is a time for everything. While I hit the stage early, at only twelve years of age, it wasn't until I was in my thirties that I felt comfortable with my sexuality. Everyone has their own path, their own story through which they go at their own pace.

Since I announced my sexual orientation to the world a few months ago, a lot of people have asked: "Ricky, what took you so long?" My answer is very simple: It wasn't my moment yet. I had to go through everything I did and live through all I experienced to arrive at the exact moment when I felt strong, ready, and completely at peace to do it. I needed to love myself. And although the process I had to go through to get to this point was neither short nor simple, I had to go through—and stumble along—my spiritual path in order to find myself.

Now, would I have wanted this moment to come sooner? Of course, especially if it had saved me from all the pain and anguish I endured. But honestly, I don't think it could have gone any differently than it did. I had to go through all this pain to really know what was inside me. I had to fall in love with both women and men, and go through each relationship to ultimately face the reality of what I was feeling. If I had decided to come out to the public when I fell in love so many years ago, it might have felt liberating at that very moment, but I am sure it would have also brought all kinds of other pain and anguish, simply due to the fact that I was not ready. The truth is that I'll never know.

WHY IT WAS SO DIFFICULT

DEEP DOWN I guess I have always known that I was gay, but I still spent many years trying to hide it, even from myself. Ever since I can remember I have felt a strong attraction to men, and though I can say I have also felt a strong attraction to and chemistry with women, it is a man who ultimately awakens my most instinctual, animal self. It is with a man that I can feel myself truly come alive, where I can find the love and passion I seek in a relationship. But I spent a lot of time resisting what I felt.

We all know people who are gay and who, for some reason, have to hide this fact in their own homes because their mother or father will simply not accept it. And even though I personally have had the full support of my family and friends, for many years the idea of coming out publicly was completely inconceivable to me. There are so many social prejudices against homosexuals that I feared people would never understand me and I would be rejected, because those were the social codes that had ruled my life ever since I was a little boy. So ever since my adolescence, when I first started to feel an attraction for men, I was struggling with the great conflict between my thoughts and my feelings.

As children we are taught, we are conditioned, to feel sexual attraction toward people of the opposite sex. When you are a little boy and your parents take you to the park and you start to play with all the other children, your parents and other relatives say, "Look how pretty that little girl is. Look how cute she is. You like that little girl?" And later you start to go to school, and when you come home in the afternoons, the first thing everyone asks you is, "Do you have a girlfriend yet?" Culturally and socially, we are taught to feel sexual attraction for the opposite sex, which causes a great deal of confusion when you feel something different. In my case, I always grew up hearing that being attracted to people of the same sex was a bad thing (for this is what many religions maintain), and I began to wage a major inner battle very early on in my life, between what I really felt and what was expected of me.

That's why I blocked it out. That's why I rejected it and employed all of my strength to fight my very own emotions. Whenever I had an encounter with a boy and felt something strong, something that shook the earth beneath my feet, I would immediately try to erase the thought from my mind. I would say to myself, "No, this isn't me. This was just a little adventure." On the one hand, I don't think I really understood what was happening to me, and on the other, I don't think I was willing to accept the fact that I didn't fit the image everyone had of me. After every relationship with a man I managed to bury my feelings, but with time this started to become too painful, as the contradiction was now too great.

But even though that contradiction was essentially in my head—and that is a conflict I eventually had to face—it's also important to understand that the rest of the world is not always filled with tolerance, the way we would hope it to be. There are many people who simply do not understand that there can be people who are different from them, and even though we may want to ignore them, we must also understand that they are a factor, and an important factor at that. Not everyone can feel at peace with his or her sexuality, because external pressures are sometimes too strong. And that, in my opinion, is tragic.

I think that one of the reasons why I found it so hard to accept myself was because in my profession I have often been considered to be a Latin idol, a pop star, and for some, a sex symbol. I don't know if it has to do with the fact that I am Latin or if it has to do with the global image of the "Latin lover," but I always had the feeling that certain things were expected of me, among which was the fact that I was supposed to seduce—and allow myself to be seduced by—women. I look at Elton John, who is indisputably an icon, and I think it's amazing how he has accepted his sexuality. But I am not he, and, culturally, I felt that the implications of accepting my sexuality in front of the world would be a lot more complicated. Maybe if there had been another artist, another Latin idol who had come before me, I might have been less afraid. But the reality is that I didn't have a role model, and that, in my mind, helped make the whole thing entirely inconceivable. I don't know if my fears were religious, cultural, or moral . . . probably a combination of the three. All I know is that for a long time, and without realizing the damage I was doing to myself, I carried around a lot of emotional baggage that precluded me from being free. From being *me*.

Looking back, I realize that throughout all of those years I lived many dark moments. I was pissed off, full of pain and self-rejection. Although on so many other levels—my career, my family, and my friends—my life was blessed with countless incredible things, there were moments when I would go to bed at night feeling the weight of the world inside as I tried to reconcile the conflicting emotions I felt. They were very painful times. It is horrible to feel you don't love yourself, and I honestly don't wish it upon anyone.

But like everything in life, pain also brings about growth. On my spiritual journey and my travels through India, and with everything I learned in my struggle against human trafficking, slowly but surely I began to find acceptance. I had to learn how to look deep inside my soul to listen to the silence and find my truth—my pure truth, free of all external pressures, expectations, wishes, and rejections. I had to learn to see and love myself exactly as I am. Now, not only can I tell the truth, but I can also talk about my pain and anger that I see as such an injustice—and not only the injustice of human trafficking, but also the injustice felt by anyone who is being judged by others. I had to understand that in the world there are people who are going to love you for who you are, and those who will want you to be exactly like them; and this simple realization hit me hard. If I don't love myself and if I hide and deny my own self, how can I expect other people to love me for who I really am? It took me a very long time to understand this.

BABY STEPS

IT WAS APPROXIMATELY five years ago when I understood and felt deep down in the bottom of my soul that I was finally ready to accept my truth. I'd had plenty of time to think, to fall in and out of love, and to live through everything that I had to live through. Until then, even though I knew it deep down in my soul, I didn't own it, and I didn't feel the need to tell it to the rest of the world. On the one hand, I felt that it was nobody's business but my own, and on the other hand, I simply didn't see how it was going to change anything. Despite the fame, and although I do seem to live a very public life, the truth is that I live my personal life very privately, surrounded by my family and the close friends that I consider family as well, most of whom have known me for decades. And since everyone in my environment already knew and accepted my truth, I didn't feel the need to tell anyone else. Besides, the fact that everything had to be done in secrecy spiced things up a bit and gave a sense of intrigue to the relationships that, I must confess, I kind of liked.

Even though I felt comfortable with the people closest to me, I think I didn't want to tell anyone else because I was afraid they wouldn't accept me. I thought, "My friends and family accept me because they love me, but what about the rest of the world? Will they judge me? Will they still buy my albums? Will they reject me?"

As an artist, one always seeks the acceptance and adoration of the audience, and therefore I was afraid this could affect my career. What would happen if I stopped selling records? What if people stopped coming to my shows? Would I have to stop doing what I love most? Today I realize how ridiculous these questions really are, but at the time I thought they were perfectly valid and important. The world has certainly evolved, and the sexuality of an artist does not have to change the way he or she is perceived. But because I was suffering, I saw only the things that scared me. And since I was afraid of coming out and telling my truth to the world, I filled myself with reasons—irrational ones, of course—not to do it.

A lot of people around me—my family, friends, and colleagues—were also afraid. Even though I know they all want the best for me, many of them were concerned about how this could ultimately destabilize me, not only from a professional point of view but also from a personal one. Many encouraged me not to do it, saying there was no need for it and that my sexuality was my business and no one else's. And even though they are right on some level, in that sentiment there is also a small dose of prejudice that I ultimately see as incredibly damaging. Despite all their advice and their love, for once I had to think about myself, and listen to what the silence was trying to tell me.

That's exactly what I did. And I was able to see my true self.

So, from the moment I accepted my own reality, I started trying to find a way to communicate it to the world. I still didn't know how I was going to do it, perhaps through a concert, a letter, a book, or a song. At the time, I had a phrase that I'd repeat to myself like a mantra: "God, Universe, or whatever you want me to call you, show me the best way to do it." I would say it to myself every day, and I kept my eyes open. My intention was to try to visualize the moment, and the entire process of this great search gradually brought me closer to my reality.

I started to make some changes. During my shows, on the Black and White Tour, I began to introduce some words and phrases that spoke to my experience. We made one video in particular in which my skin "speaks" through my tattoos, and certain words would appear, such as "accept yourself" or "change your life" or "love" or "discover yourself," "question yourself," "forgive yourself." They were words that were directed toward my audience, as I wanted to inspire these things in everyone else, but also to myself as well. I was going through a process of rebirth, and everything I did was done with the desire to wash away my secrets and anxieties so I could reconnect with the person I truly am.

When Matteo and Valentino were born, I realized how absolutely critical it was for me to find truth and transparency in my life. Even though each day I felt more and more at peace because I knew I was looking for a way and waiting for my moment to come, the birth of my sons definitely accelerated the process. When I first held them in my arms, I not only understood how beautiful and simple life could be, but I also felt the need to be completely transparent with them. I realized that what I want most in the world is for them to be able to live their lives with absolute freedom, and that no matter what, they are always proud of who they are. And to be able to teach this to them, the lesson would have to begin right at home.

I am not going to live a lie with them, and my children won't, either. I don't want my children to have to lie for me, or to go through life with their eyes covered. I want to be honest with them, so that they can in turn be honest with the world. Matteo and Valentino are my angels, my little angels, my sons, and because of them I know I'm capable of doing anything. Today, I know I have to live in absolute balance, and I have to be truly happy with who I am so they can admire me and understand that their *papi* loves them with his entire soul. If I don't do it, I will be teaching them to lie and hide from the world, rather than facing it with all the strength and pride of being themselves.

My children will grow up and eventually go to school, and now I can be at peace knowing they will never have to lie for me. When their friends ask them about their father, they will be able to explain it, without censorship and without fear. I want them to feel proud of their father, just as I will always feel proud of them, no matter what they decide to do with their lives.

This is the world I am creating for my kids—and I know there are a lot of us who are trying to forge a new generation that will know the real significance of acceptance and tolerance, one that will not know the meaning of the word "prejudice." It is a world where it doesn't really matter if you are bisexual, homosexual, or heterosexual, and everyone is simply who they are.

BATTLING PREJUDICE

WE STILL HAVE a long way to go. If the world has changed, I believe it still hasn't changed enough. It's possible that today there are fewer prejudices than a hundred years ago, or even when I was a child, but that doesn't mean that the prejudices don't continue to exist and that there isn't work still left to be done. There is a long and sad history of the persecution of homosexuals, and it is tragic to think about all the lives that have been damaged, hurt, and destroyed by the prejudices of others. I think about the great geniuses of literature, such as Federico García Lorca and Oscar Wilde, who, despite all their brilliance and the amazing legacies they left the world through their work, were persecuted because they were homosexuals. How can that possibly make sense?

Sadly, these prejudices continue to exist to this day. The media often characterizes homosexuals as one-dimensional people with no depth whatsoever, as if a human being could be reduced to his or her sexuality. The very language used all over the world to denominate homosexuals is terribly degrading: words such as "faggot," "queer," "dyke," "sissy," and others, which only serve to perpetuate hatred and discrimination among the younger generations. Because of the emotional charge they carry, such words quietly create an atmosphere of intolerance and homophobia, in which young people are afraid to be who they really are. I am not going to lie; at some insensitive point in life I also used these words to make fun of people like me. But of course I did it to "prove" to people around me that I was indeed a "heterosexual." I think you can only hate what you carry very deep down inside you. If not, why would we waste so much time on a feeling so destructive and painful as hate?

Many people continue to say they are staunchly opposed to homosexuality; they reject and repudiate it, saying that it goes against human nature. But is there anything more normal than love? What is abnormal—and infinitely cruel and unjust—is to discriminate against someone because of who they are. What is abnormal is to think that there are first- and second-class citizens, and that we don't all have the same rights.

That's what's wrong. And it is unacceptable.

Generalizations cause discrimination, and as long as there are still people in the world who are willing to label people according to their nationality, race, gender, sexuality, or the color of their hair, there will always be discrimination. That's why we have to stop it. In the same way that I never let anyone say anything negative against Hispanics, I will never allow anyone to say anything negative about the gay community in my presence. I will always insist that everyone is treated as an individual, regardless of how society may want to "label" them.

I wish I could say that I am a homosexual for this or that reason. But I can't. As far as I know, no one goes around explaining why they like the opposite sex, why they like blondes, or why they like bald people. One feels what one feels, and to try to explain it is not only futile—but wrong. Attraction does not have a logical reason. It simply happens, and as humans, all we do is react to it.

I have always thought that attraction, like love, is a matter of souls that find one another and collide. Souls aren't feminine or masculine; they simply find one another, and when there is a connection, when there is something that grabs you and turns your insides, that is when the magic is born along with attraction and love.

Love has no gender. I have been deeply in love with a man, just as I have been deeply in love with a woman. I have felt that visceral connection, that desire to always be with someone, to know everything there is to know about them, that critical need and passion for another person. So does this mean that because I am a homosexual I cannot feel something intense when I'm with a woman? No. I sincerely believe that souls have no gender, and just as I felt that my world was turned upside down when I first fell in love with a man, I have also felt a very special connection and compatibility with women. But my physical instinct, my animal instinct, and my inner desires ultimately drive me toward men. At the end of the day, I follow my instinct and my nature, period.

I remember one day, many years ago, after getting out of a relationship with a man, I said to my assistant: "No one will ever judge me for who I go to bed with."

My assistant, who was a bit taken aback because he had no idea what I was talking about, said: "That's it, Kiki. That's it. You just keep doing your thing."

Even though my sexual inclinations are not like those of the majority on the planet, I don't think this should define me any more than my preference for mango-flavored ice cream, or the fact that I have brown hair. In the same way that one should never judge people because of the color of their skin, their religious beliefs, or their ethnic origin, people should never be judged for what they do in bed or who they do it with. Sooner or later, all of us feel judged or discriminated against because of who we are, and for this reason we all have the fundamental responsibility to battle against these prejudices and make ourselves respected for who we are.

In late 2009 I read about several hate crimes that occurred in Puerto Rico and in other parts of the world; this awoke a rage in me that I can't even express. The cases were so perverse and shocking that I can only feel repulsion, indignation, and a profound desire to move mountains so that things such as this will cease to occur. The anger I felt inspired me to write a letter, which I published on my Web site and later announced via Twitter:

As a human rights activist for many years, I've been able to witness countless miracles. I've seen the amazing capacity that human beings have to heal; I've seen governments and private citizens try to change public policies and fight battles of love that have resulted in a positive impact on our society. I've seen boys and girls from different parts of the world free themselves from the bondage of human trafficking (the slavery of the new era) and amazing people renounce their "lives of luxury" to help those who need it most. Witnessing miracles of all kinds has strengthened the faith in humanity that my parents instilled in me, which is the same faith that I try to pass on to my children every day. When I watch them discovering the world, I think kindness is one of the greatest virtues that I can teach them.

On the other hand, I've also seen insufferable things that have made it impossible for me to hold on to the naïveté that I had as a child and have always tried to maintain. Traveling the world from an early age and witnessing unimaginable crimes against humanity has stolen part of the innocence that I had as a young boy. There were many moments when I forgot about the child that lives inside of me. You know, that child that we all have within and who constantly reminds us to focus on the beauty of "simplicity." But that moment of disconnection was many years ago, and thanks to the work that I do with my foundation as a part of my daily life, I'm fortunate enough to say that I have reconnected with that inner child and continue to learn from him. One of the most important things I have learned is to SHOUT to the world when I encounter injustice, and that is why I am writing today.

I try to walk through life with a positive outlook. I do all I can to keep a grateful and optimistic attitude. Call me a romantic, an idealist, or maybe someone who's just not realistic. Maybe it's a defense mechanism or maybe it's just that I'm someone who wants to change the chain of negative thoughts that have been fed to us in many ways and which can easily poison the soul. We are all human and sometimes it's easier to ignore the pain and go on with our day. "That has nothing to do with us," we may say; "Why should we care?" But today, I feel that's impossible. It does have to do with us. I do care.

In the past few weeks, I've read many articles that have made me shudder, and unfortunately the articles relate to things that are happening every day around the world. I find it almost impossible to believe that in the year 2009, we're struggling with such hateful situations.

As a defender of human rights, my goal is to find solutions for the injustices that exist in the world today. I am speaking about discrimination of any kind, whether it is because of race, gender, nationality, religion, ethnicity, handicap, sexual orientation, or political affiliation.

SO I SHOUT: WHAT IS GOING ON WITH THE WORLD TODAY?

I'm sure you all have different answers. But at the end of the day, it seems that the collective response usually comes back to one thing: "WE WANT PEACE."

Well, when we believe in peace, there is simply no room for complacency. The murders of James Byrd, Matthew Shepard, Jorge Steven Lopez, Marcelo Lucero, Luis Ramirez, and countless others who were victims of violent "hate crimes" should be completely unacceptable to every human being; because we're all human beings. It's up to us to change the paradigm. I hear the word "tolerance" thrown around in the media when it comes to cases like the ones I mentioned above. One of the meanings of tolerance is "the capacity to endure pain or hardship." Another is "the act of allowing something." To me, those don't seem to encompass acceptance, by any definition. So how about this? Instead of saying "we need to tolerate diversity," why not say, "we need to accept diversity."

Accepting diversity is the first and most important step we can take toward eliminating hate crimes and uniting humanity.

If we ACCEPT, humanity unites. If humanity unites, equal human rights will become a reality. And if equal human rights become a reality, peace will be within our reach.

At that moment I probably didn't realize that the process of writing that letter would be my training ground for the letter that was yet to be written. On the one hand, through this letter I was expressing many of the thoughts and reflections that for years had been swirling around in my head. The anger I feel when I read about hate crimes and a lack of tolerance was also a manifestation of the anger I felt toward my own history: In a way, my difficulty to accept myself also comes from my own fear of such hate crimes, and how certain people are intolerant and simply incapable of accepting anything different from them. I am blessed to have my family and to live in a world and work in an industry that is so accepting. Even though fame comes with many demands and pressures that might not be the choice of most, in the midst of it all I have the freedom to live my life the way I want to live it because, to a certain extent, fame also protects me and gives me the space to express myself the way I am. Sadly, this isn't the case for everyone else, and although the world has changed in many ways, the fact that hate crimes of this caliber continue to exist today—that in places such as Malawi, for example, there are men who go to jail for the simple fact of falling in love with a man, being a homosexual, or holding a ceremony to celebrate their union—is to me terrifying.

However, deep inside myself, a change was finally starting to happen. Instead of shaking in the face of such hate crimes, only to withdraw further into myself and keep my mouth closed, I felt the need to talk and express my indignation. Maybe it came in part from my experience in fighting against human trafficking, against abuse and exploitation, but the fact is that I decided to take action through my words.

The letter wasn't picked up by many news outlets; I'm sure there were other news stories that took precedence that day. But to me, on a personal level, a door had opened: The avalanche of support I received via Twitter was a great surprise and a total blessing. For someone like me who's used to being onstage and getting the immediate response of an audience, Twitter is a dream tool. I can write whatever I want, and immediately I get the responses and stories from people who react to what I have said, giving me their opinion or sharing in what I say. I felt so comfortable and so strong that I understood that this would be my way, and Twitter would be my tool.

THE LETTER

SO I STARTED to write. I wrote and wrote, finding a great deal of calm. At times I would feel euphoric, and other times I would cry. The process of writing was a whirlwind of emotions, because even though I knew I was doing something necessary and vital for me to be able to go on with my life, it didn't make it any easier to have to find a way to put my personal life into words.

A few days before I uploaded my letter to my Web site (and then linked to it on Twitter), I told the people around me what I wanted to do. Everyone became very nervous and instantly tried to dissuade me with all sorts of arguments: that it was not the right time, that people wouldn't understand, that we were waiting for the book to come out, that it wasn't a good idea to do it during the week of Easter. Everyone gave me a reason, and although I know that all of those reasons came from a place of love and concern for me and because they didn't want to see me suffer, I know that everyone also had his or her own reasons and fears that I hope they will one day be free of. But in this case, I was the one who was ready to get this off my chest, because now my spiritual path had come full circle.

I know that if I lose my balance, many other people—colleagues, friends, and family alike—will also lose their balance, and that causes a lot of fear. But this time, I knew I had to do what I *needed* to do and I couldn't think about anyone else. So I ignored all their recommendations, and by the end, when they came to me with the argument that I shouldn't do it during Easter because it might offend my Christian fans, I said: "What part of 'I can't take it anymore' do you not understand? What about me? In my world, my space, my 'reality,' this isn't a sin or anything I need to be ashamed of. Quite the opposite: I need to celebrate my truth!"

Martin Luther King, Jr., once said some beautiful words that I now carry close to my heart: "Our lives begin to end

the day we become silent about things that matter." On
March 29 I decided to finally put an end to the hell that
was going on inside my mind, in order to justly celebrate
my rebirth. It's about death and new life; circles are closed
and new ones opened. The only thing that mattered was
that I was ready to begin a new chapter of my life, and I
wanted to start it as quickly as possible.

And so, the letter was published. It is a text I am extremely
proud of; every time I read it I am moved remembering
everything I have faced in order to get to a point in which I
could share it with the world.

*A few months ago I decided to write my memoirs,
a project I knew was going to bring me closer to an
amazing turning point in my life. From the moment
I wrote the first phrase I was sure the book was
the tool that was going to help me free myself from
things I was carrying within me for a long time.
Things that were too heavy for me to keep inside.
Writing this account of my life, I got very close to
my truth. And this is something worth celebrating.*

*For many years, there has been only one place where
I am in touch with my emotions fearlessly and that's
the stage. Being onstage fills my soul in many ways,
almost completely. It's my vice. The music, the lights,
and the roar of the audience are elements that make
me feel capable of anything. This rush of adrenaline is
incredibly addictive. I don't ever want to stop feeling
these emotions. But it is serenity that brings me to
where I'm at right now. An amazing emotional place*

of comprehension, reflection, and enlightenment. At this moment I'm feeling the same freedom I usually feel only onstage, without a doubt, I need to share.

Many people told me: "Ricky, it's not important," "it's not worth it," "all the years you've worked and everything you've built will collapse," "many people in the world are not ready to accept your truth, your reality, your nature." Because all this advice came from people who I love dearly, I decided to move on with my life not sharing with the world my entire truth. Allowing myself to be seduced by fear and insecurity became a self-fulfilling prophecy of sabotage. Today I take full responsibility for my decisions and my actions.

If someone asked me today, "Ricky, what are you afraid of?" I would answer, "The blood that runs through the streets of countries at war . . . child slavery, terrorism . . . the cynicism of some people in positions of power, the misinterpretation of faith." But fear of my truth? Not at all! On the contrary, it fills me with strength and courage. This is just what I need especially now that I am the father of two beautiful boys that are so full of light and who with their outlook teach me new things every day. To keep living as I did up until today would be to indirectly diminish the glow that my kids were born with. Enough is enough. This has to change. This was not supposed to happen 5 or 10 years ago, it is supposed to happen now. Today is my day, this is my time, and this is my moment.

These years in silence and reflection made me stronger and reminded me that acceptance has to come from within and that this kind of truth gives me the power to conquer emotions I didn't even know existed.

What will happen from now on? It doesn't matter. I can only focus on what's happening to me in this moment. The word "happiness" takes on a new meaning for me as of today. It has been a very intense process. Every word that I write in this letter is born out of love, acceptance, detachment, and real contentment. Writing this is a solid step toward my inner peace and vital part of my evolution.

I am proud to say that I am a fortunate homosexual man. I am very blessed to be who I am.
RM

When I pressed SEND, I immediately closed the computer and went to my room to take a nap, supposedly. I closed my eyes for about half an hour, maybe forty minutes, but the curiosity killed the cat. Since I didn't want to get back on the computer right away, I called a friend who already knew what I was going to do, and I asked her to go into my Twitter account and tell me what people were saying. She said to me, "Kiki . . . it's pure love. There have been two, three, and four hundred comments—not one of them negative." Of course, there were one or two people who simply didn't get it, but generally speaking, the love I received was immediate and overwhelming. Even though deep down I didn't think anything bad was going to happen, the avalanche of love I received that day was a complete surprise. The next week my album sales even went up. Not only was I not being rejected by anybody; for all intents and purposes it looked like they loved me even more now! So all that fear I had, the fear that many people have when they come out, was only in my mind. I know this might not be the case for other people who decide to come out of the closet—I know some people encounter all the pain and suffering of rejection—but I will say that my own experience was only positive and empowering.

My family and circle of closest friends, who had already known my truth for many years, offered me their unconditional support. My father was very happy when I told him what I was going to do, as he had wanted me to do this for years, because he wanted me to free myself in order to live peacefully and openly, but he knew I had to find my moment, and he therefore supported me throughout the process until I was ready. My mother was also very happy, but the way I told her was a bit unusual.

That day, my mother was flying from Puerto Rico to Miami. I always felt that I didn't want to send the letter when she was in Puerto Rico, because like all mothers, she would worry about her son. Also, I didn't want her to be there, by herself, getting calls from everyone she knows. For the announcement, and so that she wouldn't worry, I wanted her to be here with me so she could see that her son and grandkids were all fine. So I waited until she had boarded the plane, where she would have no access to her cell phone or the Internet. When she arrived in Miami, she was picked up by one of my representatives, and the first thing they did was take her cell phone away so that she couldn't take any calls. She was dropped off at my house, and there I gave her a hug and sat her in front of the computer and had her read the letter I had just sent. As soon as she finished reading it, she stood up, gave me a great big hug, and started to cry like a baby.

A GIFT THAT LIFE GIVES ME

IT WAS AN incredible experience. Today I feel strong, happy, and free. It makes me happy to think that many of my fears—not to say all of them—were imagined or imaginary. It goes without saying that there are people out there who make negative comments and who don't understand what it's about, but I see those people as people who still have to grow and evolve, and I am nobody to judge them. Just as it took me a long time to accept my reality and accept myself, they too have yet to go through their process of acceptance and comprehension.

Someone once asked me, "When did you decide you were going to be a homosexual?" I answered, "I never decided to become anything. I simply am who I am"; then I added: "When did you decide to become a heterosexual?" Needless to say, that question went unanswered. . . .

I'm not out to change anyone's way of thinking. I am simply sharing my own experience. There might be some people who will stop liking me because they will think that until now I have not been completely sincere. Maybe others will begin to listen to and enjoy my music, now that they know who I really am. But I believe that whether they like me or not, they should do it while being aware of my whole truth. If they hate me, let it be for who I am, not for who they think I am. And if they love me, let them love me for who I am, not for who they think I am.

Today, I understand that I can't expect everybody to love me, and as silly as it may sound, it took me a long time to absorb and understand that. This enormous need I have of being accepted was very likely what led me to become what I am, because I was always willing to do what was asked of me, in order to please others. Being rejected was painful for me. That's why I kept my reality a secret. I didn't want to feel the disapproval of others, especially because on some occasions, when I had revealed my truth to some of the closest people around me, I faced some very unexpected reactions.

The thing is that we tend to perceive one another the way we want to. And when that image is destroyed, we become angry. Maybe we don't want to see the truth, or maybe we could not see it because it was hiding. Everyone lives according to a certain set of rules they learned when they were very young, many of which condition us to see the world as we would like it to be, and not as it truly is.

This is why I want to make sure that my kids grow up without the pressures and preconceptions that I grew up with. I want them to live a life without limitations of color, race, origin, or sexual orientation, and to feel total freedom to be who they are. And if tomorrow they like men or women or both, I won't be the one to hold them back or condition them to do this or that. And although I know that in life they will encounter people who will not have the open and accepting worldview they have, at least I can rest assured that they will feel peace in their hearts because they can be who they are. Needless to say there will undoubtedly come a day when they will suffer, but I hope it will never be because they cannot be themselves.

The truth is that I don't wish the pain I endured on anyone, which is why I think it is so important to fight against prejudice. Do you know how many teenagers kill themselves every day because they cannot face their sexuality? Do you know how many people grow old having never accepted their sexuality? They lead miserable lives, never allowing themselves to be who they really are. Many don't even allow themselves to discover their true nature, and to me that is a tragedy.

I would love to be able to know what it is that makes one person come out of the closet at the age of eighteen, and someone else at thirty-eight. In my case, I would have wanted it to happen sooner. But in order to find peace in the past, in that eternity that is enough to drive anyone crazy for the supposed "lost time," I have decided to accept the simple fact that it was not my moment. It took me a long time to really believe that what people think of me is not my business, that it has nothing to do with me. And every day I work to incorporate that thought so that it may become a way of life. Thinking and believing that what people say about me shouldn't be my problem has liberated me on many levels. I would be lying if I said the opinions of others have no importance in my life—of course they do—but I cannot let them define the way I see myself, making me feel less or more than what I am. What you think of me is not my reality, but instead your own. What you think of me simply isn't my problem. I found my truth when I accepted and embraced who I genuinely am. I had to battle with fear and the need to hide in order to ultimately find acceptance and to be able to love myself once again. I had to struggle with denial, with self-hate, and with negotiating with God. . . . But everything changes, I have faith.

And be it because of cultural barriers, because of how my life unfolded, or any other number of factors that played into the equation, I was not ready until I was thirty-eight. Maybe I was working so hard that I didn't even have the time to stop and think about what was really happening to me. Or maybe I wanted to hide it from myself for all that time simply because I didn't have the spiritual tools to cope with the consequences of facing my own truth. Maybe I even had to battle against human trafficking to really comprehend the injustice of what it means to steal a part of someone's life. Or maybe I had to go through the experience of being a father, to have my two beautiful angels, to be able to take a step back and understand that this is no longer just about me.

Whatever the reason may be—or maybe all of them—I am grateful for the path that has brought me to this moment, and am profoundly grateful to be who I am. My beliefs have given me enough strength that I feel protected enough to talk about this, which is a precious and beautiful thing. It is thanks to the life I have that I am who I am, that I have the children I have, and that I have the relationship with my parents I do. If I had written a letter in which

I confessed to being a criminal, that I abuse women or abuse other human beings, it would be completely out of place for me to feel so happy and liberated. But my stance is based purely on love—on love, respect, and all of the gratitude I have for the extraordinary life I have led. What I feel is so full of love, of light, of such a magical and strong frequency, that I felt I had to share it. I wanted to tell the world how proud I am of the steps I have taken, which have allowed me to get to where I am today. I sincerely wish that everyone could live, at some moment in their own personal timeline, what I am living now. It is an incredible awakening, and I wish it for everyone. It goes without saying that I am not telling everyone to be gay, but I do believe that we all carry around unnecessary secrets, things we deny ourselves because we think they are wrong. Freeing myself of my own secrets and anxieties has given me something I previously didn't know existed: emotions so strong and powerful, so transparent and amazing, that hopefully one day everyone will be able to feel what I am feeling.

To make decisions that represent significant change in one's life, we must go through many processes of destabilization, and very often we opt to stay where we are most comfortable. And that's how life goes on. But if we dare to embark on the most difficult option, we come to realize that what exists on the other side is a world of freedom, peace, and endless tranquillity.

One of the most extraordinary things about my experience has been the warmth I've received from everyone around me. I have received so many messages congratulating me and supporting my gesture, and that, to me, is a total blessing. If the subject of homosexuality is discussed around the dinner table under a different lens, that alone will make me happy. My intention in coming out was not necessarily to inspire anyone, but if on top of bringing me all the joy that it has, if my experience can serve someone else, that fills me with immense happiness. It is also a blessing to know that with my life I can benefit others, and I live that with great honor. I am proud to be who I am.

NINE

ONWARD

THE PUBLICATION OF THIS BOOK IS ANOTHER ONE OF those moments that is going to help me grow and feel stronger. The process of writing has been arduous and fascinating, and there are so many things that, if it weren't for having to put them down on paper, I might have never remembered. I made connections between events that at first glance seemed totally unrelated, only to discover that in reality they were intimately connected. I remembered, I felt, and I analyzed a lot. I discovered my own story and I fell in love with it. And maybe the most important thing is that the experience of writing this book gave me the strength and conviction that I needed to bring my truth to light. The process has been an intense exploration and acceptance, in which I have discovered myself as I truly am.

After everything that has happened—the good, the bad, the extraordinary, and the disastrous—I have finally achieved a life that is replete with light and love: I have two precious sons, a loving family, supportive friends, and an extraordinary career. And best of all, I have reached a level of peace and happiness I never even knew existed. I feel infinitely grateful to the universe, for the miraculous life I have had the great fortune to lead.

MANIFESTING

I AM OF the belief that happiness comes to those who have happy thoughts. In my mind and my heart I carry around many lovely memories that I am convinced fill my life with light, as well as with many other good things.

A very wise musician one told me:

"Drums are the manifestation of the energy and souls of our ancestors. Before, when there was slavery, the only way the slaves were allowed to express themselves was through their drums. So it's as if all those spirits that have passed away get to come back to life every time they hear a drum beating. And since they cannot dance, they enter your body and manifest themselves through your being, through you."

It is a beautiful belief and I feel that I lived it fully when I attended Carnival in Rio de Janeiro a few years ago. I had the chance to attend a parade at the Sambódromo, with one of the samba schools, and at one point during the musical rehearsals I was surrounded by five hundred drums, all beating at once. If just one drum can make you feel the power of rhythm, music, and life and you can't resist the urge to dance—imagine what it's like with five hundred drums! It was one of the most electrifying things I have ever felt in my life. For an instant you separate from your body, you let yourself be carried by the pulsating sounds, and in that moment you cease to be physical and enter the realm of the spiritual.

So if the drums are truly the manifestation of my ancestors, I can rest assured that my ancestors are with me now, because I am never too far from a beating drum!

I love that story. Because in the Afro-Antillean music of Puerto Rico—be it in candomblé, in samba, in salsa, in Native American music, or in guaguancó—drums are always present. Most religious ceremonies have drums. And this is because music has the power to liberate the mind and the spirit; it has the power to make you feel life at its most basic and natural form of expression. Music is a liberating force. Music is magical. Thanks to the fact that my life is always overflowing with music, I know I will always have a unique and fortunate existence.

And for this, I am extremely grateful.

I wrote this book while recording my sixth Spanish studio album. I had the privilege of working again with Desmond Child, and it has once again been a pleasure to feel his sense of structure, his calm, and the firmness with which he guides me throughout the creative process. The recording of an album, much like the writing of a book, is a very intimate experience. You have to sit and think, feel and allow the silence to bring about ideas that will eventually turn into sounds and words. Sometimes I start by humming a few loose notes that become a melody, and then a couple of words start to emerge. So I hold on to those words. I play with them. I toss and turn them around and start to piece them together like a puzzle. Slowly, full sentences start to appear, along with verses and stories, until they finally become something coherent, structured, something that conveys an idea or a feeling that I had never yet been able to put into words. When I start writing a song, I don't always know where it's going to go, and most of the time it takes me somewhere unexpected. A path of discovery.

The same is true for this book.

Like most of my albums, my latest is autobiographical, and it touches upon several different aspects of my life. The life I have, but also the life I want. It is a very honest and transparent record that is undoubtedly born from the renewed sense of strength I feel pulsing inside me. I have so much to say, so much to share, that I can't wait to send it out into the world and see how it will connect with the audience, with all these souls who listen to my music. I want to go on tour, get up onstage and feel the audience's energy. When I'm onstage, the audience fills me on such a visceral level, igniting me in the most powerful manner. I am happy to see how this whole process has come to be, and deep inside I know that all the days, months, and years I have ahead of me will, without a doubt, be extraordinary; I cannot wait to get there.

If there is one lesson I've learned lately, it's the importance of telling the universe what you want. If I want something in my life, if I want something in my career, or for my children or in my relationships, I have to tell it to the universe so it can become a reality. If I don't have it in my mind, if I don't absorb it and incorporate it into my life as a viable reality and not just a theoretical one, chances are it will never be actualized. I have to throw myself into the world, searching for what I want, dreaming of it, and not sitting around doing nothing, waiting for it to land at my feet like some kind of miracle.

This is very true, especially when it comes to love. You have to search for love. You have to believe in it. You have to ask the universe for exactly what you want to call to your life. But most of all, you have to be patient.

There are people in my life who have marked me very intensely. Every relationship I've been in has brought something that makes it unique and special. While one relationship might have been all about the wonderful conversations we had, everything we learned and the high level of understanding and compatibility when it came to our perspective on life, another relationship may have had more to do with the physical connection, the kind of thing that sweeps you away on a totally visceral level. Other relationships may have been more about the tenderness, the sweetness of feeling loved, taken care of and protected. . . . Whatever the case may be, no matter how difficult or torturous any of my relationships may have been in the past, I adamantly believe that true love exists. I don't know if I have already met my true love or if we are both still getting ready for the moment when we will meet. We may already know each other, we may have already been together, or perhaps we still have some steps to take before we come together. Whatever it is, all I can say is that I do know—and I know it, because in my life I ask the world for what I want—that there is a perfect person for me in the universe, and whether it takes me years, months, or days to discover him, or to realize that he is already here.

I have a very clear image in my mind of what perfect love is. Many people say to me, "But there's no such thing as perfect love. . . ." I don't care what they say; I'm a romantic! And I do believe in perfect love. I believe love never hurts. I believe love is trust, peace, calm, confidence; being playful and mischievous. In other words, for me love is freedom . . . and that is what the universe has for me. And with every step I take in my personal growth and on my spiritual path, I am getting closer. Step by step.

Regardless of what may happen in my love life, I already possess the most beautiful love of all—the love of being a father. Matteo and Valentino have brought such a powerful dimension of light, transparency, and unimaginable beauty into my life. Without knowing it, my two boys have taught me how to go far beyond my limits, and for that I will always be grateful. We often hear about the gratitude that children feel toward their parents, and even though that is very real and important, I think there is a lot to be said about the gratitude that we parents should feel toward our children, because in moments of confusion, anguish, and even joy, they are the ones who show us the way through the very love that we feel for them.

Everything I do in my life I do for them. I also do it for myself, of course, but ever since they have been in my life, I see everything in a new light. The love I feel for them is so pure, so instinctive, and so real that everything else pales in comparison. My music and my struggle against human trafficking, the importance of maintaining my spiritual north, the importance of being honest with the world . . . absolutely everything has to do with them and giving everything I can give them, and making them proud. What before seemed like an option or an alternative is now a necessity. They are my inspiration, and it is for them that I struggle to do my part to improve, because I don't want them to inherit the problems that my generation has had to battle. I want them to have the best life possible, an existence that is even more glorious and extraordinary than my own.

BETTER THAN BEFORE

IN LIFE, EVERYTHING that is good, everything that is really worthwhile, requires sacrifice. It doesn't matter if it is big or small—the fact is that we must go through countless challenges and very uncomfortable, scary moments that may bring about a great deal of suffering. But at the end of the day, when we come out on the other side, we realize that we are better than we have ever been before. It is like the process of giving birth. They say there is nothing more painful in the world than giving birth to a baby. A woman must face inhuman pain during which she may feel that she can't take it anymore, that she can't bear it anymore, that she is going to die. There is a blend of anguish, fear, and dread that something will go wrong. . . . It is an extreme moment. But ultimately she gets through the pain, she survives, and on the other side of it appears the most beautiful gift one can ever receive—the gift of life . . . and from what I have been told, the moment she holds her baby for the very first time, the pain becomes a distant thought, completely irrelevant, in comparison to the love she feels for her child.

There are some decisions that are very hard to make. But once we make them, we realize that we are stronger, happier, and more complete. We realize that we are able to do so much more than we ever imagined. Throughout the process of writing this book and baring my soul, I have learned so much. It was difficult, at times terrifying, but now I see it was a necessary step, critical for the sake of moving forward.

When I look back and think about all the angst I felt about my sexuality, and how afraid I was to tell it to the world, it makes me sad. I went through so much pain and so much tension, and now I can't believe I made such a big deal of something that now seems so simple. For a very long time I was convinced that if I came out of the closet, something bad, something truly terrible would happen. I would lose my fans, my gang would reject me, and my life would fall to the ground. But all those thoughts were based on fear, because when I came out, not only did nothing bad happen, but now I am a million times better than I was before. If someone had asked me a few years ago if I was happy with my life, I would have very honestly responded yes. But now that I have taken this extraordinary step, I realize what it means to be truly happy. I hope that everyone, in their own life, can experience a process of rebirth, an awakening such as this one. I am not saying that everyone should come out as a homosexual, but rather that everyone should make an effort to liberate him- or herself from whatever it is that is holding them back.

This is the life I have been meant to live. My story was not one where I wake up at six a.m., make breakfast, kiss my wife on the cheek, get in a car, drive myself to work, and at five o'clock drive back, make dinner, make love to my wife, and go to sleep.

My life will always be a little different from everyone else's, and I am not going to fight it. On the contrary, I am going to accept it. I do accept it. I accept it because I know that's why I am who I am today, and just because my life is not the same as many others' does not mean I cannot be happy. The Serenity Prayer says it beautifully. These are words I always carry close to my heart:

God, grant me the serenity to accept the things I cannot change; courage to change the things I can; and wisdom to know the difference.

It's true: I have to know what I can change and what I can't. My life is beautiful the way it is—why would I change it? That's how it is. I accept it and I adore it. I feel proud of it.

I believe everyone needs to accept the life they were given. That doesn't mean one should not live it as fully as possible, but ultimately what's really important is to accept and love oneself, to be happy and do good. And if you are different in the eyes of others, that is also part of your lesson in this life, because you have to learn to accept yourself exactly as you are without sacrificing your dreams in order to please others, or follow supposed social codes. *You are beautiful just as you are.* Instead of thinking, "I am different from them," try saying, "They are different from me." Anyone who is not on your same evolutionary and spiritual frequency will distance himself from you, while all those who are on the same evolutionary and spiritual frequency as you will come closer to you; you will see how amazing it is to discover that everyone who needs to be by your side will ultimately appear in your life in the most spontaneous and divine manner. That's how powerful the mind is!

My intention in this book is not to dispense life lessons to other people. I simply wanted to talk about my own life and everything I have learned along the way. If my lessons serve anyone else, this gives me great joy. But the truth of the matter is that I did this for my children and for myself. There are people who may ask themselves why I decided to write a memoir at only age thirty-eight. Memoirs are normally written toward the end of one's life, and one would hope that I still have many more years ahead of me. . . . The truth is, I feel that this is only the beginning. I have a whole new life ahead of me, and now that I am at a crossroads, I feel a deep need to stop and tell the world what I am made of. Now I realize that the most profound lessons in the world typically come in the simplest of ways. I had to see, suffer, enjoy, and live what I have lived to arrive at this place of understanding. And I want to share it with others, because I am deeply convinced that everyone can do the same. If they are willing.

Each and every one of us has to walk down his or her own spiritual path and go through his or her own karmic teachings to discover their best life possible. And for that I believe the first thing you have to do is to accept yourself and accept others. That is enough. You don't have to say anything to anyone, but you also don't have to live in the darkness. I hope that my life, and what I have written here, can serve as an example in some way. Even though my life is very particular, maybe a line or two will resonate for those who somehow feel different, whether it's because of their religion, their immigration status, the simple fact of being a minority, or for living in a country where they cannot express themselves freely.

So I choose to scream to the world: Be happy! Do good! Be afraid of change, but don't let that fear take over! And if you feel that no one loves you or accepts you, then stop and think about what I've told you here; you'll see that it's much easier than you think.

The great Irish poet Oscar Wilde once said: "A little sincerity is a dangerous thing; a great deal of it is absolutely fatal." The word he uses is literally "fatal." Wow, what a word. It makes me very sad to think that that was his experience with sincerity. I imagine he said it because he was afraid of being honest about his sexuality, especially because of the Victorian era in which he had to live. But today, in the twenty-first century, all I want is to be open and honest. It's not easy—truth is relative and it takes time to reach it. One has to make a conscious effort, every day, to live life without fear and with total transparency. Even though I have gone through everything I went through to feel the way I do today, I hope that life will continue to bless me with moments in which I am dared to go even deeper to discover something new about myself. As Pablo Picasso said, it takes a long time to be young. He was right. It takes a long time to renounce the codes of society, your faith, the laws of your home, and the laws of your country. It takes a long time to throw out all those social codes that have limited who you are, based on what has been dictated to you.

It can take you an entire lifetime until you can start from

zero all over again, without preconceptions, without prejudices, and without fear. But when you get there, and
accept who you are, you can start each day by seeing it as
it is: a divine paradise where everyone can imagine what
they want and turn it into reality. Every day begins like a
blank chalkboard, on which each one of us can write the
poem of our present and our dreams for the future.

And just as I have so many people around me who constantly inspire me and feed my soul, I also have the good
fortune of having a wonderful profession and a life through
which I can influence other people. But I know that this
privilege also comes with great responsibility. I have to be
careful with what I say and do, as it is a position I accept
with honor and respect.

With this book, I am somehow abandoning a part of my
privacy. Although there are some details and moments that
I will never tell—not because they involve something dark
or perverse, but because they are personal memories that I
prefer to keep to myself—throughout these pages I have
shown myself exactly as I am, without censorship. The truth
is never easy to pin down, especially when it is a matter of
personal truth, which is why I will always continue on with
my search, on my spiritual path, for the rest of my days. It is
this constant search that will always bring about intense
emotions. It teaches me to challenge myself, question myself,
and always push forward. But the most important thing,
and what inspires me most, is that this book can help to
inspire other people to face their fears and push forward in
their lives as well. And that is the greatest gift of all.